CITY PARKS

CITY PARKS

PUBLIC PLACES, PRIVATE THOUGHTS

Created and edited by

CATIE MARRON

PHOTOGRAPHS BY OBERTO GILI

HARPER

www.harpercollins.com

TO MY FAMILY—DON, WILLIAM, AND SERENA

CONTENTS

Introduction | CATIE MARRON

LIKE SO MANY ADVENTURES, this book started with a trip to Paris. I was twenty-three, and went there for the first time with a friend between the Christmas and New Year holidays. I remember the vibrant, white winter light, the small hotel on the Rue de Rivoli where we stayed, and our huge splurge on lunch at the old world restaurant Le Grand Véfour. And of course, walking a lot.

The clearest memory of all, the one that is etched in my mind as bright as the winter light, while all the others have dimmed, is my first visit to the Luxembourg Gardens. It was on a brisk, sunny morning, and a surprising number of people were out, most of them gathered around the boat basin, soaking up the warm sun. As I watched the scene before me, tears came to my eyes. Something about the contrast between the formal, beautiful setting and its natural, everyday humanity moved me deeply.

Each time I've visited Paris since then, I've made a pilgrimage to the Gardens. Even, if need be, as happened twice, I had to stop en route to the airport. I've grown up with this park. I used to go alone, then with my husband, and together we introduced our children to the park's grounds.

My favorite memories with them are of watching or pushing handcrafted model boats around the pond where I'd sat so many years before. One year, my husband, Don, surprised me with a small, nineteenth-century watercolor of the Luxembourg Gardens, which centered on the pond. I feel as if I can tell the exact spot where it was painted. While talking to Amanda Harlech, who wrote on the park for this book, we said we should meet at the boat pond. I mused on which of the several entrances we'd each choose to get there. I have my favorite, as I'm sure she does.

Since that first trip to Paris, I've been fortunate to visit a number of the world's most vibrant and revered cities, and I noticed after a while that I always gravitated to the nearest park. I started to look for books about my favorite parks and wondered why there were so few. On cold winter evenings, I'd dream about picking up and vagabonding around the world with my children to photograph city parks. But that didn't happen. And then this idea, which I'd quite forgotten, came back to me last year, and I began to think of a way to put it all together.

Like a winding path through Prospect Park or the Borghese Gardens, creating this book hasn't been a straight line. It's been a maze, full of delightful surprises. The most fortuitous occurrence happened very early on. I was in a bookstore and saw Oberto Gili's latest book of photographs. Many years ago, he and I had worked together on a project for Anna Wintour, the editor in chief of *Vogue* magazine, but I hadn't seen him since. Coming across his book prompted me to call him and, as this idea about a book on parks had recently come back to me, I suggested it to him. He seized on it with enthusiasm and has been the one who has traveled far and wide, to twelve countries on three continents, bringing back treasures of photographs, which form the backbone of this book.

I've tried to include most of my favorite parks and cities. Then, having those in my heart, I went about matching the right writer to the right park, that is, someone for whom the park already had deep and personal meaning. In a few instances, the writer actually preferred a different park, so we changed direction.

Just as each writer involved here has his or her own unique voice, and the photographer has his own distinct eye, each park has its own soul, one that has profoundly influenced the culture of its surroundings and the multitudes who enjoy it. Yet the parks' similarities speak to fundamental needs of urban dwellers worldwide. Parks are essential to city life, and they have been since the mid-eighteenth century, when cities became crowded and people needed an escape from the tussle and bustle of chaotic, noisy, dirty street life. They are, first and foremost, free.*

Think of how many people have made friends or encountered romance by strolling through a park, or sitting on a bench, catching a child's ball, or comparing notes on dogs. Recently, I watched a French movie, *My Afternoons with Margueritte*, based on a true story about two people of different generations and backgrounds who become lifelong friends through afternoons spent sitting in the local park. One day, the older woman reads a quote from Albert Camus to the younger man, which to me sums up what city life would be without these havens of green: "How to conjure up a picture, for instance, of a town without pigeons, without any trees or gardens where you never hear the beat of wings or the rustle of leaves—a thoroughly negative place, in short? The seasons are discriminated only in the sky. All that tells you of spring's coming is the feel of the air, or the baskets of flowers brought in from the suburbs by peddlers . . . ?"

Not long ago, I went for a late afternoon walk and iced tea with a friend. After sitting on a bench in Central Park's formal promenade, known as the Mall, we walked the equivalent of two city blocks before splitting off to go our separate directions. In that short distance, we saw men playing music, donations welcomed and received, a young man hawking jokes for a dollar, children kicking a ball, a man blowing huge, glistening bubbles using two sticks and some string, and others sitting as we just had. Curiously,

Within this collection, there are three exceptions, where fees are in fact charged: Dumbarton Oaks in Washington, D.C.; Al-Azhar in Cairo; and Xochimilco in Mexico City.

we didn't notice people on their cell phones. In the distance, I saw bicyclists and joggers speeding through the main transverse, and the famous bandshell, which people use in the morning for yoga or in the afternoon for skateboarding or on a Sunday as the starting point for a race, to say nothing of its intended purpose for performances.

Parks mirror life. After I'd written my introduction, John Banville's essay arrived. It begins with his reminiscence about his first visit to the Luxembourg Gardens. Amanda Harlech's does the same. John was eighteen, Amanda twenty; I was twenty-three. How uncanny that we referred to this experience and even mentioned our age; proof of how indelible memories of our times in parks can be. Pico Iyer writes about the outer merging into the inner, André Aciman about time, John Banville about the continuity of parks, enjoyed before all of us readers were on this earth, as well as today, and to be enjoyed, someday, after we leave it.

Parks are of the earth, they are of the people, and they give the best possible glimpse of the sky and stars amid the high-rises and rooftops of crowded urban life. They bring pleasure, and my great wish is that this book brings pleasure to you.

Al-Azhar, Cairo | AHDAF SOUEIF

CAIRO'S GREEN LUNG

A GIRL, A YOUNG WOMAN, poses. She leaps onto a marble bench and spreads out her arms. I think of birds; of flight. Perhaps that's what the young man holding the camera is thinking of too; he's down on the paving stones, his camera angled so that the background for the outstretched arms, the fluttering flowered hijab, will be the sky.

This is a piazza high above the city; a long and gracious rectangle through which water runs in a stepped canal. Dragonflies skim the water and catch the light. A little boy with an elaborately painted face jumps in. The rippling stream just covers his ankles. A guard steps forward to scold but the boy's father gently asks, "How can he see this water and not want to feel it?" The guard reluctantly steps back.

It was August, the tail end of the Eid, and it was late afternoon but still hot. The queues at the entrance to the park were long and dense: "Two adults and three little ones," "Four adults," "He's fifteen." Mostly we were Egyptian, but there were Palestinians, Gulf Arabs, Iraqis, a Swiss group . . . Soon we were through the gates and in the wide entrance square, with a hundred bubbling water jets dancing a welcome and the children squealing with delight as they ran through them, over them, into them. And suddenly it wasn't crowded, and suddenly it wasn't hot. And there were choices: Should we go right? Or left? Or a different right? Or ahead and up? Or . . .

It's odd how I still can't get the hang of the park's geography. Oh, I can look at the aerial photograph, look at the map and understand what is where, but when I'm on the ground it's easy to think myself lost. The garden, though its limits are clear, feels infinite, and in truth I am content to be lost, to wander, for a while, along lanes bordered by Indian jasmine and plane trees and our familiar Egyptian "Guhannamiyya," underhung with a purple flower I've never seen before.

Others are wandering around too. What was a crowd has become small groups, families, couples—in the seventy-two acres of al-Azhar Park there's room for everyone. The park, shaped like a giant lung, lies along the eastern boundary of Cairo, between the thousand-year-old al-Azhar Mosque and the Citadel of Salah al-Din al-Ayyubi—Saladin's spectacular twelfth-century deterrent against the Crusader campaigns rolling across the Mediterranean. The park's most public gate, the one I came through, is on Salah Salem, the motorway that connects the city to the airport. But the area has other gates accessible only by foot, opening out from the neighborhood just below the park and costing less to get through. Since the park was conceived by Karim Agha Khan as a gift to the people of Cairo, and since "those closest have priority on your good deeds," neighbors in the area can come in at half price.

Cairo, historians say, was built around a garden, and was always full of pleasure parks and amusement grounds. Hard to imagine now in a city where flora has to fight so hard for space. In chronicles from the thirteenth to the nineteenth centuries we read that the people of Cairo were fond of pleasure and "ease of heart," and that on feast days and holidays families went joyfully out to parks and other places of public enjoyment, taking boats onto the river and the lakes. Music filled the air, and everywhere there was food spread out on tablecloths and straw mats so that all who were hungry might eat.

But over the last five decades, the green spaces of Cairo have been radically eroded, and the great pleasure grounds bordering the city—al-Qanater al-Khayriyyah to the north and Helwan to the south—have more or less vanished. The riverbank is largely taken up with private establishments, and to catch a breath of fresh air in summer, people have taken to perching on bridges and traffic islands. Now, after the January 25 revolution, the people are retaking ownership of their city, spreading over every available space—and this expansion has shown just how diminished that space has become.

And so it is good to be in Azhar Park and see people walk and talk and sit and play as they must have done for centuries. I watch a family group deployed on a small hill crowned with palm trees, the bright clothes of the women vivid splashes of color against the park's green. I follow a small boy holding tight to the handles of a silver scooter, pushing against the ground furiously with one foot as he balances along the path. And there are young men and women sitting on the grass or on the low walls, looking out over the garden and over their city, making plans. And there's a security man always hovering in case a couple tries to steal more of a touch than he deems seemly, in case the current running between them sparks a fire in the bushes.

We're in transition, we say to each other, from dictatorship to democracy, from oppression to freedom. We'll get there. In an ideal world there would be no guards, no walls, no entrance fee. But in an ideal world there would be at least twenty parks like Azhar dotted all over Cairo, a park for each million of the city's inhabitants.

This is a garden that restores your humanity. It's designed to give you—at every instant—both options and the space to choose among them. Take your time and consider: will you turn right along that formal avenue flanked in ceremonial fashion by royal palms, or left and make your way up that little mound with the cunningly placed bushes and shrubs, the young couples among them bright with love and daring?

Which path is likely to surprise you? Once I turned a corner and found myself facing a huge, dreamlike lake with lazy fountains. Another time I went just a few paces down a quiet path and emerged on the top terrace of a charming, green amphitheater, its narrow, grassy steps bordered by ceramic tiles and sloping down to the pool that formed its still center.

A garden that speaks of how life should be: grace and space and options and a view. People, if you want company, but also room to be alone. There are restaurants, but most people choose to spread out picnics on the grass. There are electric buggies, but most people walk. And wherever you are you are always within reach of a bench, of a drinking fountain, made of marble, elegantly and simply carved. Azhar Park refers you to the great gardens of Islamic civilization in Andalusia and Baghdad and Damascus and Isfahan; the gardens that used the rise and fall of topography, the sounds and changing aspects of water, the varied colors and textures and characters of plants to create an aesthetic of balance and harmony.

Off the top of my head I can come up with four words for garden in Arabic: *bustan*, which makes me think of a very formal Persian garden complete with nightingales; *rawdah*, with its overtones of sport and vigor; *hadeeqah*, the most common and with the most obscure etymology; and *junaynah* (or *geneina* in Egyptian dialect), my favorite. *Junaynah* has its root in "j/n" and from this root that speaks of concealment you get *janeen* (the baby in the womb), *majnoun* (madman, whose mind is concealed), *jannah* (Heaven), and *junaynah*—or *geneina* (little heaven).

The small theater clinging to the edge of this park calls itself the Geneina Theatre. The theater is in the dip, the dry moat, between the mound of the park and the Ayyubid wall bordering its western side. The mound forms the natural slope for the auditorium, and the old, illuminated wall the backdrop of the stage, which on summer evenings sends music into the surrounding air.

It's odd to sit in the theater and think that until a few years ago this space was a giant heap of rubbish and rubble, buried under the accumulated detritus of centuries' worth of the continuous life lived here.

Walk through the narrow, busy lanes of el-Batneyyah, one of the oldest districts of Cairo. At any time and even deep into the night there are workshops humming, coffee shops flickering with television screens and crackling with the slap of backgammon counters, children playing, women buying from abundant bakeries and brilliant fruit stalls, cars inching past each other, weddings, mosques with minarets calling out to prayers. The stuff of life. You make your way through the people and the noise and the bustle and you arrive, just behind the Mosque of Aslam, at the old walls rising above the neighborhood: Salah al-Din's wonderfully uncovered walls and watchtowers rising to embrace the neighborhood. And if you're a resident of el-Batneyyah and willing to pay two pounds, you can step through the iron gate, through Saladin's walls and into the green of the Park.

A broad, widely stepped stone pathway leads you in a gentle, meandering zigzag through trees and lawns. You ascend, and your ascent reveals more and more of the city out of which you've come. Only now there's space, urban noises are hushed, details muted—here a minaret, some intricate dovecotes, the castellation of an ancient mosque, there the solid comforting form you recognize as the mosque of Sultan Hasan. The city falls away from the tenth-century wall below you, falls west toward the river, becoming a great settled, breathing mass. On good days you can see the pyramids. Every day the sun sets behind the lotus silhouette of the Cairo Tower.

And to the east, the creamy, gentle curves of Cairo's great, unique cemetery, the Qarafah, with its splendid mausoleum ruins, its courtyard featuring the eternal resting homes of the bourgeoisie, its inscriptions to poets and statesmen and artists and Sufis. The Qarafah rests in the shadow of the Muqattam, the mountain where the great stones of the pyramids were quarried so long ago. Within and around the Qarafah, the recently constructed apartment buildings tumble upward, heavily inhabited but always appearing unfinished, bare concrete arms forever held up to the sky, waiting for the next bit of money to build another level. And threading their way through it all, the two motorways that you know to be a rush of wind and noise but that from here look peaceful, their bright, moving beads of red and white car lights like silent, gliding musical notes.

The park is in counterpoint and in conversation with Cairo. It's an invitation to take a break from the city, to rise above it, into cooler, cleaner air. But it's also an invitation to contemplate the city, an invitation for the eye to wander between the parallel lines of the tall palm at the top of this hill and the mobile tower rising in opposition, among those houses across the two motorways and the cars streaming along them. What could tempt contemplation more than this position? Whether you're caught in the traffic of the motorway or struggling in the heart of the old city, the park is an invitation: a gift, an oasis, a green lung to help you breathe, to help you reorient.

Temporal and eternal life, grass and rock, motion and stillness. A lasting geography.

Boboli, Florence;
Villa Borghese, Rome |
ZADIE SMITH

TWO ITALIAN GARDENS
Boboli, Florence

WHEN MY FATHER WAS OLD and I was still young, I came into some money. Though it was money "earned" for work done, it seemed, both to my father and me, no different than a win on the lottery. We looked at the contract more than once, checking and rechecking it, just like a lottery ticket, to ensure no mistake had been made. No mistake had been made. I was to be paid for writing a book. For a long time, neither of us could quite work out what to do about this new reality. My father kept on with his habit of tucking a ten- or twenty-pound note inside his letters to me. I took the rest of my family (my parents having separated long before) to a "resort" back in the "old country" (the Caribbean) where we rode around bored in golf carts, argued violently, and lined up in grim silence to receive a preposterous amount of glistening fruit, the only black folk in line for the buffet. It took a period of reflection before I realized that the money—though it may have arrived somewhat prematurely for me—had come at precisely the right time for my father. A working life launched when he was thirteen, which had ended in penury, old age, and divorce, might now, finally, find a soft landing. To this end, I moved Harvey from his shabby London flat to a cottage by the sea, and when the late spring came we thought not of Cornwall or Devon or the Lake District but of Europe. Outrageous thought! Though not without precedence. The summer before I went to college, my father, in his scrupulous way, had worked out a budget that would allow the two of us to spend four days in Paris. Off we went. But it is not easy for a white man of almost seventy and a black girl of seventeen to go on a mini-break to Europe together; the smirks of strangers follow you from pillar to post. We did not like to linger in restaurants or in the breakfast room of our tiny hotel. Instead, on that first, exploratory trip, we found our pleasure in walking. Through the streets, through museums—but more than anywhere else, through gardens. No money has to be spent in a garden, and no awkward foreign conversation need be made, and no one thinks you odd or provincial if you consult your guidebook in front of a statue or a lake. In public parks it is a little easier to feel you belong. I felt this instinctively as a teenager (and, thinking back, as a child on Hampstead Heath). Over the next few years, in college, I found myself attracted once more to gardens, this time intellectually. I wrote my final thesis on "English Garden Poetry 1600–1900," putting special emphasis on the many ways in which "work" and "workers" are obscured in an English garden. Look at how the ha-ha replaces the fence or wall. See that solitary poetic hermit in his grotto, symbolic replacement for all those unpoetic men who dug the hole that created the artificial lake in the first place. The English lord looks out on his creation and sees just that—"creation"—unspoiled by workers' cottages or beasts of burden. With a great deal of art he has made his garden imitate nature. The window from his Surrey bedroom reveals a view straight out of a classical pastoral, apparently untouched and yet exquisite, not unlike the hills of Tuscany he spied while on his Grand Tour.

Writing that essay, I became very interested in this notion of "The Grand Tour." I read the diaries of English men of means, accounts of their travels in Italy or Germany, and followed them as they looked at and acquired paintings and statues, walked through elaborate gardens, marveled at all the marble, and stood at the base of great ruins mulling the sublime futility of existence, and so on. Nice work if you can get it. During the Michaelmas break, I visited Harvey in his one-bedroom Kilburn box and thought: why shouldn't my old man get a Grand Tour too?

But when the opportunity arrived, I discovered that my father's interests lay more in France than Italy. He liked the food and the cities and the look of the women. We wrangled a little, and I won: like all twenty-three-year-olds I was skilled at aligning any good deeds with my own pleasures. We booked for Florence. The hotel was called Porto Rosso. I understand it has recently undergone a transformation and now looks much like any other chic "boutique" hotel on the continent, but when I went with Harvey it was a true *pensione*, unchanged since the nineteenth century. Air came through windows—which we were under strict instructions to open only at night—and keys were heavy, key-shaped, and attached to giant velvet tassels. The rooms themselves were wondrously large though almost entirely empty, featuring one uncomfortable bed with scratchy sheets, one creaking wardrobe, one wicker chair, and a floor of dark red tile. No television, no minibar, no food. But you had only to look up at the ceiling, at the casually preserved remnant of some anonymous fresco, to feel what a stain it would be upon your person and nation to even think of walking down to the bellhop (no phone) to complain. True, we did not have a room with a view—unless a patch of twelfth-century wall is a view—but I was at that point in life at which even sharing a situation, albeit a poor one, with a fictional character was pleasure enough for me.

In the morning, we set out. We had the idea of reaching the Boboli Gardens. But many people set out from a Florence hotel with the hope of getting to a particular place—few ever get there. You step onto a narrow alleyway, *carta di citta* in hand, walk confidently past the gelato place, struggle through the crowd at the mouth of the Ponte Vecchio, take a left, and find yourself in some godforsaken shady *vicolo* near a children's hospital, where the temperature is in the forties and someone keeps trying to sell you a rip-off Prada handbag. You look up pleadingly at the little putty babies. You take a right, a left, another right—here is the Duomo again. But you have already seen the Duomo. In Florence, wherever you try to get to, you end up at the Duomo, which seems to be constantly changing its location. The heat builds and the walls of the alleys feel very high; the thought of a green oasis is now as tantalizing as a cold bottle of water, though far more difficult to attain. The last time you remember seeing grass was that little strip in front of the train station. Will you ever see it again?

En route, we tried to amuse ourselves. Harvey, a talented photographer, snapped pictures of beautiful women as they dashed from shade to shade; I, far less able, took a poor shot of a piece of ironic graffiti: *Welcome to Disneyland, Florence.* It got hotter. "Where *are* we?" I asked my father. "The Piazza of Fish," he muttered, but then he was struck with fresh vision: "I've a feeling we should have crossed that bridge." I remember this small geographical insight coming over us both as a revelation: there was, after all, a way out of this oppressively beautiful warren of streets, and it led to higher ground. Height being the essential sensation of Boboli. Climbing toward it, we felt ourselves to be no longer British rats running round a medieval Italian maze—no, now we were heading up into the clear, entitled air of the Renaissance, to triumph over the ever-moving Duomo, once and for all. Through formal gardens we passed, each one more manicured and overdesigned than the next, our cameras hanging dumbly from our necks, for Boboli is a place that defeats framing. As an aesthetic experience it arrives pre-framed, and there's little joy to be had taking a picture of a series of diametric hedges. "It's not much like an English garden, is it?" ventured Harvey, confronted by Bacchus sitting fatly on a turtle, his chubby penis pointed directly at our foreheads. In one lake, Poseidon stood naked about to stab a trident into a rock; in another, a fellow unknown to us reared up on his horse, as if a sea that had once parted for him now intended to swallow him whole. I remember no ducks or wandering fowl, not a leaf or pebble out of place. In Boboli you don't really escape the city for the country, nor are you allowed to forget for a moment the hours of labor required to shape a hedge into a shape that in no way resembles a hedge. Boboli is Florence, echoed in nature. It is a piece of public oratory, spoken by the Medici clan and still perfectly audible through the centuries. *Not only can we bend popes and painters to our will—we can also bend bark!* No, not like an English garden at all . . . though perhaps more honest in its intentions. It speaks of wealth and power without disguise. As a consequence of this, it is the only garden of which I can remember feeling a little shy. I would not have thought it possible to feel underdressed in a garden, but I did— we both did. Clumsy tourists dragging ourselves round a private fantasia. For though Boboli may be open to the public, it is still somehow the Medicis' park, and the feeling of trespassing never quite leaves you. Not that the garden isn't magnificent—of course it is. But in the humble opinion of the Smiths, it lacks "hidden gems." Everything is laid out for your awe and admiration. It was a relief to find ourselves for a moment on an avenue of curved yew trees, shaded and discreet, where we were offered the possibility of respite, not only from the awful sun, but from the gleaming of monuments and the turrets of villas. I think we were too English for Boboli. The English feel a garden should have a little privacy in it, a few bowers as well as bravado. Sometimes the bark should bend in quietude, not just in vulgar display.

At the very peak we rested, and took far more photos of the red roofs of Florence than we had taken of the gardens themselves. "Very grand, that was," said my father, a little later, when we had descended into a not-grand-at-all café to happily eat a baby cow covered in tuna sauce. Seeing his relief I thought sadly of E. M. Forster's Charlotte Bartlett, and heard her grating voice echoing in my own mind: *I feel that our tour together is hardly the success I had hoped. I might have known it would not do.*

VILLA BORGHESE, ROME

A LITTLE WHILE AFTER MY FATHER DIED, I moved to Rome. I was in mourning and it was winter, and the city was all stone and diagonal rain to me. I had no sense at all of it being a green place. I walked past the Spanish Steps into the wind without wondering where they led. With the spring, small patches of green revealed themselves: the ring of grass around the Castel Sant'Angelo; or the little walled garden off Via Nazionale, dotted with defunct fountains, one deep, waterless well, and covered in the scrawls of teenage lovers. RAFAELLA—TI AMO! We would never have found these spots if not for the dog, who sniffed them out. One day in April, under a hedge in this walled garden, my husband led our pug to something more melancholy and curious than a pine cone: an empty Statue of Liberty costume, a tin of green spray paint, an empty bucket, an Indian immigrant's identity card.

It took us a while to discover the Villa Borghese. We lived on the other side of town, which is to say, less than fifteen minutes away, but of all the parochial spots in the world, Rome is one of the worst. Each *rione* is so charming and self-sufficient, you rarely feel the need to adventure beyond it. I should think we were in Monti a year before we crossed the river to explore the relative wilds of Trastevere. Once again, the dog provided impetus. By the summer she had helped pull us anxiously toward the Italian language, where we did our best to keep up with the chatter of the other dog owners we met in the walled garden, exchanging veterinary tips or boasting about bloodlines. (I never saw a mongrel dog in Rome. They all looked like they'd come straight of out of the "Breeds; Canine" section of the encyclopedia.)

"E dove possiamo corriere con il nostro cane senza guinzaglio?" I tried, and was rewarded, despite my grammar, with an avalanche of friendly yet almost totally incomprehensible information—verbs running into adjectives at high speed—yet from which we were, in the end, able to pluck a few nouns. The best place to run a dog off the lead was in a bourgeois villa. And where was this middle-class villa? Why, up the Spanish Steps! We'd see a villa and then a park. There would be museums and bicycles and lakes and a zoo, which is not called a zoo but a *bioparc. Che assurdo!* And yes, dogs, everywhere dogs. There is a special place for dogs!

THE BORGHESE GARDENS ARE SHAPED like a cartoon heart, though only a map reveals this: when inside, you walk its winding arterial paths without any sense of a formal plan, surprised here by a café, there by a lake, here by a museum or a film festival, by the head of Savonarola or a carousel or a wild splash of lavender. It is a lovely example of a truly public park. Wrestled from the fists of a sixteenth-century cardinal and his descendants (who opened it to the public on Sundays and public holidays), it was delivered, in the twentieth century, into the hands of the people. Like Hampstead Heath, like Central Park, it has wide avenues on which to promenade, and high grass in which to read and kiss, and children and dogs are welcome to run wild—though in both cases they are better dressed than their London and New York counterparts. Once we saw a borzoi in a yellow raincoat, yellow rain hat, and four yellow booties. On Sundays you get little girls with a lot of froufrou curls and bows and underskirts, and boys in blazers and ties, like the tiny CEOs of Fortune 500 companies. At the spot we had been told about—where dogs may run without leads—things were more casual, though the Roman fetish for that British sartorial horror the Barbour jacket was everywhere in evidence. ("We are out in the open air, like an Englishman," these jackets seem to say, each to the other, "exercising our dogs as the English do.") Towering Italian stone pines create a luxurious canine obstacle course; classy hounds chase each other in figures of eight while their owners laze about on a natural slope, and settle in to watch people conduct their private lives in public. *It Happened in the Park* is the English title of Vittorio de Sica's lovely 1953 movie (in Italian it was simply *Villa Borghese*) and that's how it is: as if the doors of everybody's apartments have fallen off and left a clear view for any passing stranger to take in. In the six separate vignettes that make up that film, de Sica trumpets the glories of voyeurism, while celebrating the power of the segue: his vision of a public park is of a journey without maps. In life, as in the film, one arrives with a very particular plan—a picnic in a precise spot, or a visit to the gallery—but the park is so full of random temptations and opportunities it will always thwart your ambition to get from A to B. In one vignette, a couple of Roman prostitutes on the run from the law stumble across, and enter into, a Miss Cinema beauty contest taking place in the park. The message: anyone can make it in the gardens of the Borghese. And it is this easy transition between high and low that is central to the charm of the place. It does not exclude. That all those stone busts of famous men should have their names clearly printed beneath, for example—well, it may be only a small matter of nineteenth-century taste, but what a difference it makes. One does not wander around nervously, ashamed of a lack of knowledge. Any housewife can walk right up to da Vinci and think: what girlish cheekbones! How weird they look with that great beard! Any working stiff can eat gelato in front of Archimedes, peer into his stone eyes, and consider how much he looks like old Giancarlo from the post office. Harvey would have loved all that.

There is a sentimental season, early on in the process of mourning, in which you believe that everything you happen to be doing or seeing or eating, the departed person would also have loved to do or see or eat, were they still here on earth. Harvey would have loved this fried ball of rice. He would have loved the Pantheon. He would have loved that Rossetti of a girl with her thick black brows. In the first season of mourning there is a tendency to overstate. But still I feel certain that this was the garden that would have made us both happy. It was a bittersweet thing to walk through it without him, thinking of our last trip together, to crowded, expensive Venice, which had not been much more successful than Florence. Why had I never thought of Rome? Like me, he would have loved the glimpses of the new arrivals: African families, Indian couples, Roma girls hand in hand. Sitting for a picnic, unpacking foods that smelled wonderfully of coriander—a herb most Roman grocers wouldn't know from a weed. Harvey and I knew from experience that it takes a while for an immigrant to believe a park is truly public and open to them: my mother always used to complain, exaggerating somewhat (and not without a little pride) that she was the only black woman to be seen pushing a stroller through St. James Park in 1975. Sometimes a generation of habitation is needed to create the necessary confidence; to believe that this gate will open for you too. In Italy, where so many kinds of gates are closed to so many people, there is something especially beautiful in the freedom of a garden.

FOR OUR TWO YEARS IN ROME, the Borghese Gardens became a semi-regular haunt, the place most likely to drag us from our Monti stupor. And I always left the park reluctantly; it was not an easy transition to move from its pleasant chaos to the sometimes pedantic conventionality of the city. No, you can't have cheese on your *vongole*; no, this isn't the time for a cappuccino; yes, you can eat pizza on these steps but not near that fountain; in December we all go to India; in February we all ski in France; in September of course we go to New York. Everything Romans do is perfect and delightful, but it is sometimes annoying that they should insist on all doing the same things at exactly the same time. I think their argument is: given that all our habits are perfect and delightful, why would anyone stray from them? I suppose they have a point, but it is still a relief to escape into their gardens and eat food in any order while sitting in the grass and drinking a British amount of alcohol without anyone looking at you piteously. In a public Italian garden a Briton has all the things she loves about Italy—the sun, the food, the sky, the art, the sound of the language—without any of the inconvenient rules that attend their proper enjoyment. She is free to delight in that incredible country on her own slovenly terms. To think about her father and how he would have loved these oily *arancini* that she bought near the Pantheon (which he would also have loved). To watch the people come and go. And then perhaps go boating. And then perhaps fall asleep, a little drunk, in the grass.

When my father died I dashed to Rome leaving a lot undone. I'd packed what little I found in his room in a box and abandoned it in my basement. Two years later, when I returned, I had to go through his things properly. There was not much, but there were some photos of these final trips we'd taken together in France and Italy. I think he got some pleasure from those holidays, but the photos have a sort of dutiful air to them, as if he's taking them to please me. He liked to get them blown up and sent to me in a large padded envelope, perfect as postcards and equally uninteresting. The only sublime shot was taken in France, in Carcassonne (his choice), where he quite uncharacteristically demanded a car stop so he could walk back a few yards to the edge of a sheer drop that gave on to a view of a valley. Here he took a magnificent panorama, of hills and dales and forests and fields, and a little thread of blue running through it all. He never sent me that one, but I found several copies of it among his things after he died, as if he didn't want me to know that the gardens he liked best were the wild ones.

Dumbarton Oaks, Washington, D.C. |
PRESIDENT BILL CLINTON

ONE OF THE MANY WONDERFUL THINGS about Dumbarton Oaks Gardens is the pervading sense of surprise—surprise at what you see when coming upon a gate or around a hedge, something you missed on a previous visit. Explore the grounds a dozen times and you'll find a dozen fresh pleasures: a quote carved into a stone wall, a design woven into a brick footpath. Poke a bit into the garden's history and the names you unearth—Edith Wharton, Alger Hiss, Andrei Gromyko—will surprise you as well.

My first visit to Dumbarton Oaks was as a college student at Georgetown in 1964. While I had visited Washington, D.C., as a delegate at Boys Nation the year before, it was only after moving to the city that I began to get a sense of its special mix of political intrigue and history. The garden was peaceful, as it still is now, a place to settle onto a bench with a book and forget for an hour or two about life outside the wrought-iron gates.

Now when Hillary and I stroll through the terraces and down the winding footpaths, I realize that the aura of history is unmistakable. Like much of Washington, Dumbarton Oaks is a mix of orderly Europe and untamed America. Since the garden is built onto the side of a steep slope, much of it is terraced, bordered into rooms and sectioned by hedges and brick walls, but it also contains sloping lawns dotted with fruit trees or forsythia. As you make your way on some of the lower paths, the main house on the hill above is hidden from view, and the air is so quiet you can only hear the water from a fountain, or from the small stream below the gardens in the more untamed national park that shares Dumbarton's name.

Just as in other great urban gardens, a wonderful mix of people find themselves sharing this common—and uncommonly beautiful—setting. Hillary and I have met people from all over the world at Dumbarton Oaks, mostly curious tourists who introduce themselves, tell us where they're from, politely ask for a photo, then continue their wandering and leave us to ourselves.

For a history buff like me, the origins of the garden are nearly as interesting as the garden itself, particularly the story of two women who created it: Mildred Bliss, its owner and matron, and Beatrix Farrand, the landscape architect Bliss hired in 1921 to transform the wild and neglected fifty-four acres at one of the highest points in Georgetown into a majestic estate. At fifty years old, Farrand had already designed nearly a hundred private gardens and public spaces, including portions of the grounds of Yale and later the White House, but Dumbarton Oaks would become her most enduring masterpiece. Of the three designers in her office assigned to work on Dumbarton Oaks, all were women; in fact, for a time every single designer in her office was a woman.

Mildred Bliss so trusted Farrand that the architect hired to build the great house, Franklin White of McKim, Mead & White, had to get Farrand's approval on any exterior features before presenting them to the owners. For Bliss, the exterior details of the structure would have to suit the gardens, and not vice versa.

But the house also comes with its own unique history. In 1944 it was the site of the Dumbarton Oaks Conference, a meeting of Allied diplomats to plan what was to become the United Nations. They needed a cool place within the mostly unair-conditioned city of Washington, and a rising State Department employee named Alger Hiss—who would become famous in later years when he was accused and tried for being a communist spy—recommended the house and gardens, which Mildred Bliss and her husband had by then turned over to Harvard University. Diplomats from the

United States, Great Britain, and the Soviet Union worked at the estate for more than six weeks. The young Soviet ambassador who attended, Andrei Gromyko, would continue at or near the helm of Soviet foreign policy through five premiers and nine presidents. He was such a tenacious negotiator that Henry Kissinger once said, "If you can face Gromyko for one hour and survive, then you can begin to call yourself a diplomat."

Most days during the conference the ministers would have lunch on the main terrace high in the gardens, or in the orangery when it rained. One of the participants related in his memoirs that some of the most contentious problems were resolved during these meals, when tensions were naturally lower. The conference held in the great rooms at Dumbarton Oaks wasn't entirely successful, but I believe that the agreements reached must have been helped along by the view of the beautiful gardens below.

Whenever Hillary and I visit Dumbarton Oaks, we enjoy both the garden and thinking of the strong women who created it, the world-changing discussions that took place there, and the unique place it holds in the history of our capital, our nation, and our world. Something surprising lurks around each corner—someone with a fascinating story who came from far away to visit; or every once in a while, a young man or woman, resting on a bench, peacefully absorbed in a book.

Giardino Pubblico, Trieste |
JAN MORRIS

AT THE TOP OF THE ADRIATIC SEA, where Italy meets Slovenia, stands the fine old port city of Trieste, and in the heart of Trieste is a public garden, Giardino Pubblico Muzio de Tommasini.

In most cities, parks and public gardens add to the luster of a place, contribute handsomely to its effect, advertise its history, or proclaim its style. Not the Gardino Pubblico Muzio de Tommasini in Trieste. For one thing, hardly any visitor sets eyes on it. For another, few of us know who Muzio de Tommasini was. The garden is no more than a cramped enclave of greenery, hemmed in by bustling city streets, seldom crowded even by its own citizenry, and dismissed by most guidebooks in a couple of lines.

But the allure of the garden is this: that far from showily exhibiting to the world the character of its parent city—like Central Park in Manhattan, say, or Dublin's majestic Phoenix Park—it has quietly absorbed the city's character into itself, and has become a true microcosm of the deeper civic meaning. Trieste is intensely proud of itself, but not in a flaming way. Muzio de Tommasini was no dazzling general or revolutionary statesman. He was a distinguished local botanist and the eponym of a well-known crocus, *Crocus tommasinianus*. But more important, in this context, he was also mayor of Trieste, and his garden is above all a garden of municipal Worthies.

TRIESTE IS A DELIGHTFUL AMBIGUITY. It is a leftover, so to speak, from the Austro-Hungarian Empire of the Habsburgs, who ruled the town for several centuries and made it their chief outlet to the Mediterranean—in effect the port of Vienna, and one of the great seaports of the world. Standing as it does on an ethnic fault line, it was at once Italianate, Slav, and Germanic, and when the Habsburg empire died with World War I, it rejoiced in the Risorgimento and became part of Italy.

Its glory days were over, though. It had lost its European purpose, and it has never quite found another. The Tommasini Garden, founded in 1854 in the prime of the empire, is a memory of the city's bourgeois climax—a memory, not a memorial, because there is nothing elegiac about it. Nineteenth-century Trieste was fundamentally a merchant city, made wealthy by its port and attracting men of visionary enterprise from all over the world. Like Manchester in England, built upon cotton, or industrial Chicago in Illinois, it became a city of intellect, too, whose style was proudly set by a cultivated cosmopolitan bourgeoisie. It is a public loyalty that lives on in Mayor Tommasini's garden.

THE GARDEN GREETS YOU with an uncharacteristic bombast, as you walk there up the ever-tumultuous Via Cesare Battisti (perhaps having stopped halfway for a coffee at the Café San Marco, a haunt of Triestine worthies to this day). For suddenly there, where the road bisects and the garden is about to begin, you are confronted by a startling statue. It portrays the most prominent Trieste intellectual of his day, and one of the most influential citizens: Domenico Rossetti, who died in 1842. He was the Father of All City Fathers, philanthropist, lawyer, scholar, littérateur, patron of the arts—the Triestino par excellence.

High on a plinth, around which female Allegories (Archeology, Poetry, Jurisprudence) precariously reach up to honor him, Rossetti clasps a book in one hand, while the other is held to his heart in exclamatory mode. A long bronze cape theatrically hangs around his shoulders, added by the sculptor to hide the fact that Rossetti was slightly hunchbacked. But it makes for a masterly effect, and geometrically lined up behind the statue, too, is a bare-breasted bronze Trieste in the very act of liberating herself from the claws of the Austrian eagle.

Breathe easy, though; that's the end of flamboyance. Once you are past Rossetti in his grandiloquence, Trieste in her triumph, you are liberated too. You are in the garden proper now, and all around is green foliage and complacency.

THE GARDEN IS, I SUPPOSE, three or four hundred yards long, but that's just an estimate. It feels oddly expandable to me, like a dream garden in *Alice in Wonderland*, sometimes intimate, sometimes big enough to get lost in. It is entirely surrounded, by splendid trees, as Tommasini would doubt-less have wished it—pines, ilexes, laurels, a cork tree, a Spanish fir, a cedar of Lebanon, a sequoia, sundry species less recognizable to me—an arbo-retum handsomely guarding the perimeters of the enclave, and giving it a Victorian sense of dignity. Through their branches you may glimpse the incessant traffic passing by outside. Above the whisper of their leaves you may hear a contemporary rumble of cars. But if you choose a bench some-where among the flower-speckled, bee-hummed, butterfly-haunted clover lawns, acclimate to your surroundings for a while, and then set off in gentle exploration, you are liable to feel comfortably nineteenth century yourself.

THERE IS NOTHING DISCORDANT to this garden. Meandering around and across it, with many more benches thoughtfully disposed, narrow paths lead you through shrubberies to its varied conveniences. There is a station of the Third District Municipal Police to keep an official eye on the deco-rum, a pompous little part-yellow building that is a living reminder of the

Habsburgian governing manner. There is a small roller-skating rink among the bushes, and a tennis-table court with stone tables, and a glade floored with a chessboard, and a modest children's playground, a quiet duck pool with a fountain statue of Leda and the Swan, and at the very top of the park, out of the trees, a café with al fresco tables.

The chances are slim that you will find anybody behaving in an indecorous way, or for that matter roller-skating, ping-ponging, or even playing chess. You may meet one or two fellow wanderers, though, and children skipping around the pond, watched by quietly gossiping mothers, and you will certainly come across solitary souls sitting on benches, sleeping, meditating, writing love letters, reading tattered books, or incuriously watching you pass by. There will be a few morose-looking gulls around the pond, and a duck or two, and possibly a skulking black cat. Rooks will caw, sparrows will twitch, perhaps you will see the flicker of a lizard on the wall of the police station. And at a café table there may well be a serious group of elderly ladies, some with the blue-rinsed hair of yesteryear, deep in a game of cards, while one of their group keeps the score in a diligent script on a notepad (I know—I've looked over her shoulder . . .).

All this, to my mind, speaks of satisfied well-being. This garden is civilized, cultivated, and pleased with itself. It is not one of your aristocratic pleasances or honky-tonk parades, neither a Coney Island nor a Rotten Row, but a proper place of pleasure for a proud and successful middle class. And that is why long ago the Trieste municipality made it a Garden of Worthies.

WHEREVER YOU STROLL in the Tommasini Garden, Worthies on plinths confront you, in bronze or in marble, sometimes dotted starkly on an expanse of lawn, sometimes with little flower gardens of their own. You cannot escape them. Emerge from some shady bower into the sunlight and lo, there is a Worthy stern before you. Lose your way in the shrubbery, and a Worthy will be around the corner to set you straight. Drop your chocolate wrapper on the grass, and be sure it has not escaped the notice of a Worthy. Sometimes they suggest to me miniature Easter Island figures, but they are really Trieste entablatured.

There are perhaps two score of them, by my last befuddled count, including one woman, and they are placed there to commemorate, in particular, their contributions to the cultural and intellectual distinction of their city.

As it happens they do not look like a very merry lot. I smile hard at them often, but like their Easter Island confreres they seldom smile back. They include musicians, artists, poets, scholars, educationalists, a botanist (Tommasini himself, in a place of honor), Italo Svevo, and James Joyce (portrayed within a sort of bronze picture frame, perhaps to show that he was only a visitor with a passport . . .). Bearded or spectacled, one or two of them hatted, however disparate they were in life, in sculpture they are united in symbolism.

Not all their names, I fear, will be familiar to most of us, but as a collective they are endearing—slightly comical perhaps, but touchingly inspiring, too, in their love for their city, and their pride in it.

FOR THEY ARE NOT JUST THE WORTHIES, but actually the Virtues of old Trieste, embodied here once and for all in their green and ordered garden, with the ducks and the birds and the occasional lizard, with the ladies at their cards and the loungers on their benches, all among the dark green foliage, tolerantly oblivious to the world outside their garden.

Gorky Park, Moscow; Tsarskoe Selo and Kirov Park, St. Petersburg |
IAN FRAZIER

MOSCOW—ST. PETERSBURG

THE FIRST TIME I WENT TO RUSSIA, in July 1993, I could not believe the weeds. They grew to great heights along the road into Moscow from Sheremetyevo Airport, and climbed the steps of the crumbling, moss-covered footbridges we went under, and seemed to reach almost to the second stories of the ramshackle Soviet-era apartment buildings in the suburbs, and fringed the lower regions of the steel girders of the huge tank-trap monument marking the farthest point of the Nazi advance during the war. Moscow's spring must have been rainy; these were some serious weeds. Cow paths wound through them and women went into them while minding goats and looking for mushrooms. The only place where I could see that the weeds had been knocked back at all was on the small apron of a church where a workman was cutting windrows with a scythe. With the recent fall of communism everything had changed, nobody really knew what would happen next, and the weeds gave the city a wild and unbarbered look that went well with the sense of chaos.

I made that first trip in the company of Russian artist friends who had left Russia for America fifteen years before and had not been back since. For them the return was nerve-racking and marked by sudden spills of emotion. The Moscow Institute of Contemporary Art and an arts group in New York had combined to sponsor an exhibition about Soviet statues and what should be done with them. The best-known image from that exhibition was Art Spiegelman's revision of the famous communist statue of two workers, a man and a woman, striding forward into the future; his sketch suggested that the pedestal be moved farther back so that the workers appeared to be stepping off into empty air. For my friends, Vitaly Komar and Alexander Melamid, this was the first public viewing of their work in Russia since they were kicked out of the artists' union, before their emigration. With Katya Arnold, the artist wife of Alex Melamid, I explored Moscow on foot for days at a time, and the statuary theme of this trip made me extra aware of statues. Maybe even the passing pedestrians were thinking about statues then; we went by a Russian guy who was standing in front of a statue of Nadezhda Krupskaya, the wife of Lenin, and giving her a good cussing-out. Katya said the guy did not omit personal details, like Krupskaya's froggy eyes, and then he descended into language too disgusting to translate.

The show consisted mostly of pencil sketches and various mock-up images and it was held in a dim corner of a cultural center that resembled a parking garage. The grounds of this place were all weeds, too, and among them, as if put there for raw reference material, lay many recently toppled statues from the communist regime. At that time I knew little about the icons of Soviet power. I was told that a seated figure now tipped over flat on his back and staring at the sky was Yaakov Sverdlov, the Bolshevik leader and comrade of Lenin and Stalin who was thought to have ordered the killing of the czar and his family in July 1918. This was the first I'd heard of him. Though several times larger than life size, he looked mild enough in stone, with his rimless spectacles and short beard.

There were others—oratorical Lenins, now prone or supine, some with a gesturing hand still raised as if they had just thought of one last thing to say, and a pink marble Stalin tipped over on his side, and one or two guys whom even my Russian friends couldn't identify. If I had been better informed about the Cold War the thought might have occurred to me that I was walking among the enemy dead. But like most people, I suppose, I respond better to the purely personal.

For me the personal part kicked in when we were walking along a main avenue and I saw a towering, dramatic sculpture in a roundabout up ahead. Katya said it was the memorial to Yuri Gagarin, the cosmonaut. As we approached the statue it looked almost comical, with the first man in space portrayed like Astro Boy above a skyward swoop of something unidentifiable, maybe rocket exhaust. I had a moment of clarity and predicted to Katya that the date at the base of the statue would be in April. I guessed this because my father, a scientist, had been upset about how the Russians were outstripping us in rocketry, and I remembered playing in the yard on the first nice day of spring and coming into the front hall to find Dad hanging up his coat in a state of deep discouragement. I asked what was wrong and he told me the news about the Gagarin flight. He said the Russians were simply better in science than we were, and we would never catch up to them. I took this as a dig at me, because of my lack of aptitude for math or science. Suddenly the bright spring day had turned to gloom. I could even remember the light green jacket I had on. When Katya and I got up to the statue its base bore the date of the Gagarin flight—April 12, 1961.

Past the Gagarin statue we continued down the avenue and came to an entrance to Gorky Park. All I knew about it back then was the Martin Cruz Smith novel of that name. It's a great thriller, but somehow it had left out the weeds. Maybe they were a more recent thing. If Moscow appeared overrun with weeds, Gorky Park, I now saw, must be where they originated. In their rush to spread out into the city they flourished so luxuriantly along the park's boundaries that one had to look to see that there was, in fact, a wall or a fence in there. Sometimes they almost met above the footpaths. In an area that had once been an amusement park none of the rides seemed to be functioning, and the weeds had claimed pieces of broken machinery and taken over. We hurried through, past trash and drunks and vaguely sinister loiterers.

On a later visit I stayed at the apartment of Alex Melamid's mother while she traveled in America, and because it was on Leninsky Prospekt, which ran by Gorky Park, I sometimes wandered into the park on long jaunts to and from the city's center. Going along the park lanes I stepped carefully. A quick look into a weedy byway might reveal something unforgettably sordid. One or two of the awful images of Russia that I can't get out of my mind appeared to me in Gorky Park. But in the following years, the city cleaned up the park and restored the gardens and mostly got rid of the weeds. Across the street from the main entrance planners laid out a big promenade area called the Graveyard of Fallen Monuments, and some of the sculptures I had seen by the cultural center ended up there, along with many other deposed statues and monuments. I don't know if they're still there today. After a few years of traveling to Moscow I decided the better city for me would be St. Petersburg.

I liked St. Petersburg because, in the first place, it worships writers. No other city makes shrines of famous writers' former dwellings the way St. Petersburg does. In the course of my visits I saw where Dostoyevsky, Blok, Akhmatova, Nabokov, and Leskov had lived. Sometimes, too, I would come upon elaborate markers honoring writers I had never heard of.

At the apartment building in which the poet Joseph Brodsky was a teenager, I found the outside now bore a plaque with a large bust of him in bas-relief profile. Brodsky and his parents occupied a partitioned-off allotment of forty square meters in a communal apartment with three other families, and his parents remained here until they died. He wrote about this place in his essay "In a Room and a Half." I checked out the bust and thought it a fair likeness. I had met Brodsky once, in my publisher's office. At the time he was in declining health—near-starvation during the blockade permanently damaged his constitution—and he had a greenish pallor. He was sitting on one of those little gray chairs for visitors that editors wedge into their offices among stacks of books and manuscripts, and he reached up to shake hands, barely registering me. I had read nothing by him then. After he died I finally did read his work, and I wondered at my luck in having met him. He is the only person in my life whom I have seen both in the flesh and as a statue.

As I got deeper into Russia, took more trips there, and even planned to take a car journey across Siberia and write a book about it, my Russian friends said, ruefully, *"On zabolel Rossei."* Conventionally that would be translated as "He fell in love with Russia," but what they really meant was closer to the verb's root, *bolet'*, "to fall ill." I had fallen ill over Russia. I now see the long episode partly in terms of a midlife crisis, humdrum as that is. I studied Russian history and sort of learned the language and read Russian books in English and (a few) in Russian. My stacks of notes on Russia grew into heaps. To my friends who had been unable to stand life there and had emigrated, I appeared to be on a mysterious, perverse track. But to new friends I met in Russia, I seemed no crazier than any American—they had none to compare me to besides the ones they'd read about or seen in movies or on TV—and they were willing to put up with my indifferent language skills and show me around.

Through Boris and Sonya Zeldin, longtime friends of my wife and me, I got in touch with Sonya's childhood friend Lyuda Sokolova, who had a comfortable small apartment near the center of St. Petersburg. On trips longer than a few days I rented her apartment while she stayed in another that she shared with her husband and his mother. Her husband was ill and could not work; Lyuda worked at the Russian equivalent of the city zoning board. Her salary was small. She told me that when she retired in a few years her pension would be even less. She spoke no English and had never been out of Russia, and when I suggested she come visit us in New Jersey she replied that she had looked into the price of a ticket to New York and she could afford it only if she did not eat or drink for one year. Like every Russian I knew, she was a tireless walker, and she sometimes accompanied me on explorations.

The entire city of St. Petersburg itself could be described as a shrine to Alexander Pushkin, the country's best-loved writer. He lived most of his life in that city and left traces of himself all over; I went around collecting Pushkin-related sightings and locations. I read his poem "The Bronze Horseman," and then contemplated the imposing statue of Peter the Great on horseback that had inspired it; I paused outside a restaurant with a plaque claiming that Pushkin used to stop there for coffee; I noted the giant gold Pushkin profile above the stairs at the public library when I went there to read about him. On spare afternoons and weekends I did all the official Pushkin things there were to do—visited his apartment on the Moika River and saw his book-lined study and his pen-and-ink sketches and his beaver hat and the bloodstained waistcoat he was wearing when he was shot, and the anonymous letter (in facsimile) that called him "King of Cuckolds" and provoked him to the fatal duel. I stood with a reverent tour group before the couch on which he died.

Any fan of Pushkin must also go to Tsarskoe Selo, the imperial palace, gardens, park, and village built during the mid-eighteenth century in the woodlands about twenty miles south of St. Petersburg. Pushkin attended school at the Imperial Lycée in the village of Tsarskoe Selo from when he was twelve until he was eighteen; it was his only formal education. Later he and his wife rented a dacha in the village. Court life in St. Petersburg tortured Pushkin and probably contributed to his death, but Tsarskoe Selo gave him great happiness. He wrote, *"Nam tselyi mir chuzhbina / Otchestvo nam Tsarskoe Selo."* ("For us the whole world is a foreign land / Our fatherland is Tsarskoe Selo.") Because of Pushkin's influence, later poets used the place as a retreat. Akhmatova wrote much of her work there in the early twentieth century and famous verses by Mandelstam describe it as a kind of paradise.

Lyuda and I took a Tsarskoe Selo tour bus from Nevsky Prospekt on a Saturday morning in mid-January when the air was so cold that tiny pieces of frost hung like suspended glitter. We had dressed warmly, Lyuda in a hat of fur dyed a deep burgundy. Except for me all the passengers were Russians, including young kids and teenagers. The quiet respect with which even grade school groups in Russia will listen to docents talking about Pushkin is unlike anything I know of in America.

Russians, as it seems to me, always favor the orthodox approach—they've been Orthodox Christians, orthodox Marxists, orthodox atheists, and now orthodox followers of modern-day crony capitalism. When they fall for a belief they don't mess around; they go all the way. Passionate as they have been about these systems, what they really believe is deeper and survives all creeds that come from outside. The true, deep-down Russian religion is animism. Russians believe that things in the world possess individual spirits of their own. This applies to any tree, plant, place, machine, or object of any kind. When I asked the laconic, sad driver who picked us up that first time at Sheremetyevo Airport how his very used car was running, he replied, "Is an old man ever well?" A woman who was showing me how to dial her telephone once explained to me, "He likes to be dialed *slowly*." The clock in Lyuda's apartment announced every hour in a sprightly female voice—"The time is eight o'clock exactly!" She called the clock "my auntie." Windshield wipers are "janitors," alarm signals chirp like sparrows, and the term for speed bump is "lying-down policeman." And so on.

Baba Yaga, the famous old-lady witch of Russian fairy stories, had a house with chicken legs on which it could jump up and run around. Similarly, most buildings of significance in Russia are seen as animate beings. Often they embody the spirit of the ruler in power at the time they were constructed. You will be told that a building is an Ivan the Terrible building, or an Alexander II building, or a Brezhnev building. Stalin-era buildings or projects—the huge swimming pool he ordered to be dug on the former site of the largest church in Moscow, for example—not only may be said to represent Stalin, they sort of *are* Stalin. His spirit will inhabit them forever. On a smaller scale, there's a category of special, individual spirit that is believed to occupy a house or an apartment. This spirit is called a *domovoi*. When an object falls in an empty room or a window rattles suddenly, that's the *domovoi*. Sometimes when people emigrate to America they worry about what will become of their *domovoi*, which can ride along in the household goods but is unable to cross water.

Our tour guide on the bus—a slim, well-dressed woman wearing the crisply pleated gray wool slacks favored by Russian lady professors—was talking too fast for me to follow. I asked Lyuda what she was saying and Lyuda answered, "Nothing, really." The bus left St. Petersburg and crossed mostly empty regions of hedge lines, small villages, and snow. Soon it slowed down in the village of Tsarskoe Selo and pulled into the parking area near the three-hundred-yard-long Imperial Palace. The guide was saying something about how Peter the Great began construction of the buildings and parkland at Tsarskoe Selo in 1710, and how the architect Bartolomeo Rastrelli designed the palace in the 1740s. To my mind, the basic and most important fact about Tsarskoe Selo is that Empress Catherine II, known as Catherine the Great, still reigns as its resident spirit. Catherine's sense of baroque, Germanic splendor (she was a German) informs the palace and its blue-and-gilt façade and its ballrooms and its famous Amber Room, and her whimsy enlivens the naturalistic English-style landscape park, to which she added a miniature Chinese village and a pyramid to mark the burial ground of her dogs.

Our minibus drove around the immense expanse of park beside the palace, but the deep layer of snow made it difficult to admire the landscape design. The guidebook said something like "statues on classical themes diversify the view," and I had noted several interesting ones that I wanted to see. That the season happened to be winter made the goal better. Outdoor statues in Russia must collaborate with snow for four or five months of the year, and I like the way even the most thuggish sculptural monstrosity looks with snow draping it and icicles hanging in unflattering areas. Here at Tsarskoe Selo, however, I was in for a disappointment. Each statue on the grounds now resided in a little wooden boxlike covering of unfinished boards, evidently to protect it against the weather. This was taking animism a bit far. Famous works like the *Girl with a Pitcher*, *Discobolus*, and *Galatea* had retired for the winter into small huts of their own.

Pushkin's lycée, the part I'd been waiting for, came at the end of the day. Over our shoes or boots we put on those canoe-shaped felt coverings called *tapichki*—most Russian museums insist that you wear them, ostensibly to protect the floors but also maybe just to make you feel dumb—and then we fell into shuffling step behind a young Asian woman guide. Her Russian was slower and easier for me to understand.

For me the lycée brought to mind hardscrabble academies in middle-of-the-country American towns just after the frontier had moved on. Like those start-ups the lycée had been a hick school, far out of any European mainstream, yet also rigorous and sophisticated in its way. The dorm room that Pushkin once occupied had his name on the door. His classmates shared in his fame just by being in the same school; like characters in a buddy-movie fantasy, each student in the immortal crew also had his name on his door.

Although the Nazis never got into St. Petersburg, they trashed Tsarskoe Selo and other palaces and historic places outside the city. Photos of the destruction, on display in many museums, are even more striking when compared to the meticulous and thorough job of restoration done by the Soviets. Like all the guides I'd listened to, our young woman leading our tour detailed the "fascist" damage perpetrated here. The Nazis stripped and burned the building so that nothing remained but the shell. What is now the building's interior is a replica based on historic paintings and photographs. When postwar reconstruction of Tsarskoe Selo began, the first window in the entire village to be replaced was the one in Pushkin's room in the lycée.

Eventually I did drive across Siberia (with two Russian guys I met in St. Petersburg), and I made other trips there, and I did write the book, and it came out. I thought my interest in Russia might end with that but somehow it carried on. I made no other trips, but I kept reading about the country and following it in the news. A YouTube video of Vladimir Putin singing "I Found My Thrill on Blueberry Hill," for example, magnetized me so I could not stop watching it. And of course I followed the protests, and the fascinating Pussy Riot story. And I've been reading a book called *Russian Criminal Tattoo Encyclopaedia*, which has lots of wild photographs.

Recently I was at a dinner with a woman named Irina who was among those I met in Moscow on my first trip, back in 1993. She is married to the brother of my friend Katya. One of the reasons I learned Russian was so I could talk to her husband, Mitya, and her. Irina reminded me of a drunken evening we'd spent at someone's apartment when a few of the guests started making disparaging remarks about Americans. I remembered the evening, but not the remarks, because I hadn't understood anything at the time. Yes, Irina went on, the people there expected me not to understand. But then, she recalled, everyone was surprised when in a loud voice I pronounced, *"Provolochnoe zagrazhdenie tanki protivniki ne priiduyt!"* During the intervening years I had forgotten about that sentence. It was the first I learned to say in Russian, and it means "The enemy tanks will not cross the barbed-wire entanglement!" I memorized it before that trip as a kind of social icebreaker and interesting Cold War thing to say. Irina recalled that after I said it and again fell silent the other guests eyed each other nervously, then confined themselves to pleasantries for the rest of the evening.

As for my friend Lyuda, her life took several turns in the years after our trip to Tsarskoe Selo. She retired from her job with the zoning office and received a pension higher than she'd expected, thanks to Putin's reforms. Her poor husband's illness became untreatable and he died. Through a friend of Boris and Sonya, who had introduced me to her, she met a man named Yuri when he was visiting in St. Petersburg. Yuri was from Leningrad/St. Petersburg originally. He had immigrated to America in the 1980s, married, and become a U.S. citizen. Now he was divorced with grown-up children. Yuri and Lyuda began to see each other. Eventually they married. Yuri had made money in banking and after the wedding the couple traveled widely and then settled in Livingston, New Jersey, about a half-hour drive from my house. I have breakfast with Lyuda from time to time and we often talk on the phone. She still speaks no English and I still don't understand a lot of what she says. Here in New Jersey, we have become good friends.

Griffith Park, Los Angeles |
CANDICE BERGEN

AT 4,300 ACRES, GRIFFITH PARK is not a park in a city; it is a city in itself. It began, in 1896, as an ostrich farm. No, let me start over. It began as a natural anomaly: a shady, stream-fed canyon where indigenous peoples held tribal meetings. They called it "Moco-Cahuenga."

You know how this story goes. When the Europeans arrived, the area morphed into Rancho Los Feliz, which was then bought by a Welshman named Colonel Griffith J. Griffith, whose name some might call redundant.

Griffith turned the land into an ostrich farm to provide plumage for women's hats. As legend goes, when he began to be stalked by the ghost of Antonio Feliz, the former owner, and feathers fell from favor, he donated the land to the city of Los Angeles, which named it, for obvious reasons, Griffith Park.

Griffith Park quickly became a mainstay location for film production, beginning with another Griffith, D.W., who used it to stage battle sequences in *The Birth of a Nation* in 1915.

John Ford shot there; *Back to the Future* used it; *The Terminator*, *Who Framed Roger Rabbit*—some part of Griffith Park is used virtually every day of the year for film and television production.

In fact, when I was a child one of the cowboy stars at the time built a museum called the Gene Autry Western Heritage Museum, which is on the eastern border of the park. The park is home to the celebrated Griffith Park Observatory, which was a key location in the well-known film *Rebel Without a Cause*, starring James Dean and Natalie Wood. In fact, there is a bronze bust of James Dean at the entrance.

The park houses the Los Angeles Zoo, the Greek Theatre, three golf courses, twenty-seven tennis courts, and Travel Town Museum (to which my father donated a steam engine). It has a Bat Cave, Bronson Canyon, Captain's Roost, and fifty miles of riding and hiking trails.

It overwhelms. But not with beauty; it is not that kind of park. It was not designed by noted landscaped architects nor planted with exotic Latin-named plants. It is splayed in a semi-desert smog belt and covered with scrub brush and the odd stands of eucalyptus. It does not enthrall or provide serenity for contemplation. What it mostly provides is dust.

If there was ever a jewel in this park's crown, it was the minuscule retreat called Fern Dell. The microclimate of Fern Dell became popular with residents who flocked to drink from its natural spring, calling it "the Fountain of Youth" until it was made obsolete by the invention of cosmetic surgery.

This was a part of the park with which I was well acquainted, because when I was a child, my maternal grandmother used to take me there to feed the ducks. It was a verdant, luxuriant dell in a city not known for sheltered nooks and I loved our outings there. Except for one thing: my grandmother, whose name was Lillie Mae and who was from the Deep South, had incredibly pale skin of which she was very proud. Skin so white it was on the cusp of blue. She zealously avoided the sun and often, in order to protect her porcelain complexion, she resorted to extreme measures.

She would take the brown paper bag that held the bread crumbs we had brought for the ducks and would fashion it into a hat that she put on her head while holding my hand.

The most recent royal wedding introduced Americans to the millinery term of "fascinators." Well, this was a "humiliator." You can't imagine. In fact, the only other person who can is my much younger brother, who when I mentioned that Nana used to wear a paper bag as a hat, said, immediately, "Ralph's."

"Who's Ralph?" I asked.

"It was a Ralph's Market paper bag. It was at the La Brea Tar Pits and it was horrible."

Same hat. Different venue.

She would roll the bag up a couple of times, giving it a kind of brim or cuff, I suppose, and perch it jauntily on perfectly coiffed red hair while I turned beet-red with shame.

She looked like a half-baked Little Dutch Girl.

Just as this memory is seared into my childhood brain, so is the perfection of Fern Dell. The fireworks of ferns bursting from walls of rustic stone. Fifty species of fern in as many shades of green blending into cushions of mossy fur. The soft sound of water rushing over terraced stone and guppies darting in and out of crevices; the twined faux-bois bridges with over-fed ducks paddling beneath them; the sound of children laughing at my grandmother.

As I grew into my teenage years I entered the realm of Horse Transference; the fifty miles of bridle trails in the park became my new recreation spot. From one of the many stables that ringed Griffith Park, we would rent the saddest-looking horses. Truly, they were sway-backed, dull-eyed, matted beasts whose job was to carry young idiots around the large, looped main trail.

When I finally cajoled my parents into getting me my own sway-backed, matted beast, I moved from riding at Griffith Park to a private stable farther away, and only returned occasionally to ride in horse shows. I didn't really see the park trails until years later, when I was asked to do a movie about a horse race, *Bite the Bullet*. The cast was asked to meet at the Equestrian Center to choose a mount since we would be spending most of our time on horseback. I arrived early and selected a large, dappled gray gelding. We got to try our horses out on the trails outside the Equestrian

Center, crossing the bridge over the tiny trickle that was the Los Angeles River.

The trail took us up into the mountains overlooking the San Fernando Valley, which, unusually, was not obscured by smog. The other actors were solid, responsible riders, and we were out an hour and a half. When we returned, our horses were loaded onto a trailer to start their trek to Nevada, where we would begin shooting.

When my daughter, Chloe, was six, I decided she should learn how to ride, so every weekend I would bring her to the tony Equestrian Center for lessons. She never showed much interest in horses, but I thought riding might be a good mother-daughter activity. She was bored witless by horsemanship classes so I suggested she try vaulting, which is, basically, performing gymnastics on the back of a slowly cantering horse. I thought the high-risk aspect would perhaps engage her. Alas, these lessons lasted only a couple of months as well.

Another phenomenon I discovered at the Equestrian Center was team penning, an event that took place every Wednesday evening during the summers. This was a rodeo event in which a team of riders separated one cow from a herd. It pitted genuine cowboys from affordable, earthquake-prone Sylmar, which was zoned for horses, against newly hatched equestrians from Bel Air and Beverly Hills.

Many had gotten their new payloads from highly lucrative television careers, and buying overpriced quarter horses and hand-tooled leather tack was one way to express their wealth. I would see celebrities in fringed-suede, violet custom-made chaps riding a slickly groomed horse and talking intensely on cell phones. Gucci cowboys.

They would meet up with the authentic cowboys and cowgirls who trailered their horses more than an hour from their houses and together they would enter the ring while country music played over the loudspeakers. Real riders with old, worn saddles would team up with the Recent Riders whose shiny horses wore silver rosettes on bridles of hand-woven rawhide and together, this misfit group of cowboys would single out one cow from the herd trucked in every Wednesday. It was a parallel universe all its own and it existed right in Griffith Park.

The last time I rode in Griffith Park was two years ago, when my daughter, then a budding journalist, had an assignment to interview mega country music star Taylor Swift for the cover of *InStyle* magazine. Ironically, my daughter's idea was to take Taylor riding. I still don't understand why. But she asked if I would help find a stable, so I did and went ahead to wrangle the horses. Taylor and Chloe arrived in Taylor's enormous Escalade SUV with a massive security guy who was not going anywhere near a horse. This is how I found myself on a sway-backed, dusty, dull-eyed beast just like the ones I originally rode as a young girl, as we set out to ride the same looped trail.

Recently, my husband and I visited Fern Dell. I had not been there in sixty years. Perhaps the memory of my grandmother's hat kept me away. The years have hardly been kind and the landscape was barely recognizable. The series of gently cascading falls no longer ran with water. Instead, it was clogged with black sludge. No ducks. No guppies and no ferns. Of the more than fifty varieties of fern that had once thrived there, there are now none—they have been pilfered by the many visitors who had taken them as souvenirs.

There are still, of course, many visitors. Korea Town is next door to Fern Dell and groups of Asian women wearing cross-trainers were out for a hike that day. Many Hispanic families walked through the pocket park and several hip young couples from the trendy, adjacent section of Los Feliz pushed their babies in strollers.

Evidently, Fern Dell is about to be rehabilitated. It couldn't be too soon.

Rejuvenation, after all, is in this city's DNA, and the whole of Griffith Park is constantly inundated with visitors, filled every weekend with Angelenos taking advantage of the vast resource. Lines snake down the mountainside waiting to get into the observatory. Tennis courts and golf courses are packed. And Griffith Park remains the best spot from which to view the iconic HOLLYWOOD sign. In case you forgot where you were . . . as if such a thing were possible.

Grosse Tiergarten, Berlin|
NORMAN FOSTER

PARKS ARE A VITAL AND HUMANIZING part of the infrastructure of our cities; they are critical to the health and well-being of urban dwellers. By creating a sense of place, they often symbolize the very identity and soul of the city. To paraphrase Gertrude Stein, they ensure that "there is a there there." Often a park is more than emblematic of its city—it is a time capsule that can chart the flow of change over generations. This historical dimension is nowhere more manifest than in Berlin's Tiergarten, whose story is inseparable from the turbulent background of its capital.

Berlin is Germany's greenest city, with more woods and parks than any other metropolis. The Tiergarten has the distinction of being Germany's first public park. Covering 520 acres (210 hectares) in the heart of the city, this makes it one of the largest in the world. By comparison, the entire state of Monaco covers just 480 acres (198 hectares) and would fit comfortably within the park's boundaries.

Before focusing on the Tiergarten, however, I would like to put the idea of a city park into the wider context of civic design. The flight from the countryside to the city is a global phenomenon, yet there is no accepted model for these new or enlarging urban communities. At one end of the spectrum there is the dense, traditional city, where the emphasis is on walking or public transport. On a sliding scale this ranges from medium-density examples such as Berlin, Copenhagen, and London to ultra-high-density cities such as Manhattan, Monaco, and Hong Kong. At the other extreme, there is the low-density, car-reliant city with its sprawling suburbs, such as Los Angeles or Detroit.

IN ANY DEBATE ABOUT THE MERITS of urban versus suburban living, access to greenery is a major positive of suburbs, though the virtues of a private garden are countered by the burden of commuting. Paradoxically, greater densities in a city often combine a desirable lifestyle with higher property values. In most examples, proximity to a park or garden square adds to real estate value.

The unique DNA of a city is inextricably bound up in the nature of its green spaces. London has its origins in a collection of villages. Over time these communities fused together, but each retained its own identifying green focus. The destinations on London buses spell out this diversity—Shepherds Bush, Hampstead Heath, Islington Green, and Primrose Hill, to name but a few. This diffusion amounts to a system of parks, large and small, spread across the metropolis. It is the polar opposite of the centralized park, such as one finds in Manhattan.

In the same vein, Tiergarten reflects Berlin's history. Between 1900 and 1920 Berlin's population doubled to four million, making it the third-largest city in the world, after New York and London (by the time of reunification in 1990 it would be less than a quarter of that peak). In the 1920s, Berlin was the most industrialized city in Europe, with the most advanced transport infrastructure—Tempelhof Airport opened in 1923 and the S-Bahn was electrified. It was also home to the avant-garde artists, architects, writers, and composers of the day. The English diplomat Harold Nicholson captured the vitality of the pre-war city in this extract from 1929:

> There is no city in the world so restless as Berlin. Everything moves.
> The traffic lights change restlessly from red to gold and then to green.
> The lighted advertisements flash with the pathetic iteration of coastal

lighthouses. The trams swing and jingle. The jaguar at the zoo, who had thought it was time to go to bed, rises again and paces in its cell. In the Tiergarten the little lamps flicker among the trees, and the grass is starred with the fireflies of a thousand cigarettes. Trains dash through the entrails of the city and thread their way among the tiaras with which it is crowned. For in the night air, which makes even the spires of the Gedächtniskirche flicker with excitement, there is a throbbing sense of expectancy. Everybody knows that every night Berlin wakes to a new adventure.

Five centuries separate Nicholson's thousand urban fireflies from the pastoral hunting grounds of the electors of Brandenburg, when the Tiergarten (literally "animal garden") was a silent deer preserve. Its transformation from forest to park began in the early eighteenth century, as Berlin assumed the scale and ambition of a capital city.

In 1742, when Frederick II ordered the perimeter wall to be torn down and the Tiergarten opened to Berliners, the architect Georg Wenzeslaus von Knobelsdorff began the process of creating a garden. Marshland was drained, watercourses created, and parterres and mazes arranged in the late-Baroque manner. "Salons" for discreet social gatherings were screened by hedges and furnished with seating and fountains.

Under Knobelsdorff's successors, the gardens were gradually reworked in the English landscape tradition. In the early nineteenth century, Peter Joseph Lenné recast the Tiergarten as a *Volksgarten* for use by a growing population, overlaying the Tiergarten's avenues with a filigree of footpaths to create a bucolic landscape of meadows, lakes, and watercourses amid dense clusters of trees. Strategically located statues—which together constitute a remarkable body of work—commemorated German heroes and celebrated the arts.

It is this diversity of form and the shifting moods it evokes, depending on the time of day, the quality of the light, and the changing seasons, that makes the Tiergarten so special. The visitor can discover everything from forest wilderness to manicured lawns, from long vistas to the fine detail of its statuary. In part, this breadth of possibilities is made possible by the park's incredible size; walking through its woods, one really does feel removed from the city. However, its success ultimately rests on the skill of its designer.

Over time, the only major changes to Lenné's idyll came in the form of nationalistic memorials, chief among which was the Siegesallee (Victory Avenue), laid out in 1873. This broad boulevard ran south through the Tiergarten from Königsplatz (now Platz der Republik), where the gigantic Siegessäule (Victory Column) was erected. Lined with statues—a veritable "hall of fame" of Prussian history—the Siegesallee became a popular promenade. It was during this period that the Reichstag was built on the edge of the park, close to the Brandenburg Gate. Designed by Paul Wallot and completed in 1894, its four-sided glass dome dominated the skyline from the Tiergarten, symbolizing German imperial might.

Nothing remains of the Siegesallee now. Like Königsplatz, it was swept away in Hitler and Speer's rush to drive their North-South Axis through Berlin as part of their fantastical plans for Welthauptstadt Germania. Charlottenburger Chaussee, which formed part of Speer's East-West Axis, was widened and inaugurated in April 1939, in time for Hitler's fiftieth birthday. The Siegessäule was uprooted at the same time and moved to the Grosse Stern, where it still stands.

The Tiergarten under the Nazis assumed a role suggested by Knobelsdorff's "salons"—a place where meetings might be had away from prying eyes and ears. In the early years of Nazi rule the daughter of William Dodd, U.S. ambassador to Germany, noted how the park's fashionable riders and strollers were joined by officials reluctant to be seen meeting formally. Dodd himself met people in the park until he realized that "even in this lovely and romantic setting," Nazi informants followed him.

BY THE END OF APRIL 1945, having reached the western edge of the Tiergarten, Soviet Marshal Zhukov trained his artillery on the Berlin Zitadelle, two miles away. With Zhukov's progress through the park, the final act in the Battle of Berlin began. Symbolically, after the fall of the city, when the Red Army erected a monument to their dead they placed it on the site of the Siegesallee. It was erected so hurriedly that it ended up in West Berlin, outside the Soviet Zone.

When I first visited what was then West Berlin, it was a democratic oasis in a communist desert. I recall piloting a Piper Navajo, flying low through the narrow air corridor that connected the city with the "free world." The threat of MiG fighters looking for trespassers required me to have a copilot with local knowledge of the terrain alongside me in the cockpit. Seen from above, the Tiergarten offered a guiding green hand.

A pilot flying over the Tiergarten in the months after the German surrender would have found a different scene. Not only was the city in ruins, but the park itself—then in the British sector—was a wasteland, its trees felled for firewood by Berliners unable to find coal, its meadows cultivated as allotments. The wholesale dumping of debris in its lakes was only prevented by the intervention of Reinhold Lingner, head of the Berlin Central Office of Environmental Planning, who effectively saved the park. In March 1949 Mayor Ernst Reuter planted a linden tree to mark the start of a reforestation program and gradually the park began to regain its pre-war form. Over the next ten years 250,000 saplings were donated from across West Germany. Deliveries even continued by plane during the Berlin Blockade, tracing the same route into Tempelhof that I followed on my first flight.

Landing at Tempelhof then provoked contradictory reactions. On one hand I was exhilarated by the bravura of its sweeping curve and cantilevered roof, which sails heroically above the aircraft. I have since described it as "the mother of all airports." But entering, I recall a sinking feeling. Its echoing halls seemed saturated with historical associations, inevitably evoking its fascist roots. Years later, visiting the Reichstag for the first time conjured a similar range of emotions.

The fall of the Berlin Wall in 1989, and German reunification, marked the final phase in the history of the Reichstag and the Tiergarten. An international competition was launched in April 1992 to transform the Reichstag building into a parliament for a unified Germany, moving the seat of government from Bonn to Berlin. Eight months later three practices were short-listed, one of which was Foster + Partners. I presented our revised proposals in June 1993 and shortly afterward we were announced the winner.

Over the next six years I traveled to Berlin monthly and got to know the Tiergarten intimately. I walked its paths and watched it change with the seasons—rhododendrons in bloom in summer, skaters on its lakes in winter. I particularly remember one freezing February, when we were conducting a lighting experiment with a model on the roof of the Reichstag, gazing out across the park and seeing its naked trees, Giacometti-like against a deep blanket of snow.

Three aspects of our design changed the appearance of the Reichstag dramatically. One was the glass cupola with its spiral ramps and elevated viewing platform. It has given the public a new relationship to the Tiergarten, as they can view the park stretching below them. It has also enabled a new relationship between public and politicians. Raised symbolically above their representatives, people can now look down onto proceedings in the assembly chamber. In its previous life the Reichstag was entered through a little side door. But through the reinstatement of the original West Entrance, with its neoclassical portico, the building has been reconnected to the ceremonial green space of the Platz der Republik—the scene of historic gatherings in the past—and beyond that to the Tiergarten.

In a controversial move, I sought to have the scars and graffiti on the walls inside the old building preserved for posterity. The dialogue between new and old played out within the Reichstag found its equivalent in the Tiergarten. Dilapidated buildings on its edges, abandoned after the war, were given new leases on life; embassies sprang up; and competitions for a new German chancellery and administration buildings followed. Out of sight, a combined road and rail tunnel was formed beneath the park, part of a drive to renew Berlin's transportation infrastructure.

In the thirty years since I first visited Berlin, the transformation has been dramatic. It is almost impossible to compare the city now to how it appeared when divided by the looming presence of the Wall. Although the city retains a uniquely gritty quality, it has virtually reinvented itself. Amid this changing scene is the constant presence of the Tiergarten.

High Line, New York |
ANDRÉ ACIMAN

For Annapaola Cancogni

THEN AND NOW

THERE IS A MOMENT—and it seldom lasts more than that—when the High Line wears two seemingly incompatible faces: old face and new face. One needs to catch the fleeting alignment of the two, but there is never a guarantee that it will happen, and hoping that it might, or even trying to make it happen, could easily ruin the spell. But unless that alliance does happen, the High Line remains either a leafy, new promenade frequently overlooking the Hudson, or a refurbished elevated rail track that was once destined for demolition. The very neighborhood around the High Line, which recently bounced from grubby blue-collar to high-end gold coast, reflects the tale of this Janus-faced fusion, where a once-rotting, 1.45-mile-long, elevated eyesore, built eighty years ago over Tenth Avenue, can within seconds morph into a suspended high-tech, new-age, eco-friendly, cutting-edge green park where all of us must, each in our own way, eventually confront the insoluble enigma of *then and now*. What was then, what is now.

You walk along the High Line and let your hand glide along its lean, painted steel railing, which spells the latest in near-futuristic design, and yet, scarcely within reach across the way, you'll spot Edward Hopper's red-brick building or his timeless portrait of Manhattan's rooftops with their wooden water tanks jutting out from a ziggurat of rooftops where more barrel-shaped tanks wear their pinewood, pointed hoods. As I catch myself thinking of Hopper, I am equally reminded of New York's other painter, John Sloan, who died the year I was born, and whose paintings suddenly come alive each time I'm on the High Line. For there they are: the same homing pigeons flying over a roof—they haven't changed since Sloan painted them a century ago; the same drying laundry struggling to shrug off its clothespins as a wild autumnal storm blusters in on Manhattan; and the same old Chelsea with its dappled sunset beaming listless orange over an unseen Hudson. There, too, this morning as in Sloan's world, the solitary figure of a woman steps out onto a roof terrace to air her thoughts.

This *then and now* moment may last a second—not even, perhaps—but on paper, as I let my mind distend the fantasy, it begins to acquire a life of its own, so that even if my impression of John Sloan's spirit hovering over today's New York is short-lived, or even a touch contrived or exaggerated by the lacing and cadence of words, its dilation on paper creates a reality, a tale that becomes as good as real. I can think back on the moment when thoughts of Sloan first raced through my mind. Better yet, I can take these thoughts home with me, knowing I'll look back on them someday.

This is Sloan country. If while staring north on the High Line, I can no longer dispel John Sloan, and if John Sloan intrudes on my vision, then his paintings have become the visual equivalent of a soundtrack. We bring music wherever we go these days and allow our iTunes to inform our impressions of urban life. We carry remembered images, too, and project these onto the city the better to see the city before us. But above all we seek and we bring time, wherever each of us finds it and however we cobble it onto the present. We do so not only to see what's before us but to see *other* and therefore to see *more* than what's just before us. We see things that are only partly there, or almost not there, but that we know mean more to us than what our eyes behold. We look to remember what we thought we saw.

Without real or imagined traces of time, without the inflection of memory, or of something that borrows the circuits of memory, and passes for memory, but may not be memory at all, we'll never see, much less understand, what lies before us. It is time that confers meaning to the High Line;

time is the film we bring to everything we wish to see when we hope to amplify what our eyes are seeing. Time dilates the senses. Time is about the footprint, not the foot; the luster, not the light; the resonance, not the sound, the trace, not the thing. Time is how we fantasize, privatize, and ultimately seize and understand the beauty of what lies around us.

Then and now.

When you lean against the High Line's railing and stare at the view from what was the trellised old El, it is about time that you want to think. I walked under the High Line exactly twenty years ago after leaving a dinner party on Horatio Street. The High Line was a defunctive, rat-infested, overgrown rail yard on its way to extinction. Now, two decades later, I am back but in no way can remember what the area was like once. Probably so ugly that I didn't even care to look around. All I wanted was to get into a cab and head home. Now the ritzification of this once-dingy meatpacking district has reached dizzying proportions with luxury hotels, boutiques, art galleries, and restaurants sprouting just about everywhere around the High Line.

Meanwhile, the swanky, jet-setty bar scene spills over the glistening cobbled streets at night and the chatter of glitterati and fashionistas is so loud you forget that this was once an industrial, working-class area that emptied out at night. Past sundown, this was prostitute alley. Correction: transvestite prostitute alley. From the windows behind Horatio Street where I was frequently a guest, we would turn off our lights, stare outside, and watch the meatpacking area ply its other trade. On New Year's Eve we drank champagne and we cheered.

THE HIGH LINE WAS BORN IN 1934 and for almost fifty years served as the fastest and most efficient way to bring "meat to the meatpacking district, mail to the Post Office, and agricultural goods to the factories and warehouses of the industrial West Side." Because it ran through several warehouses, it facilitated the speedy delivery of goods and merchandise by avoiding the use of Tenth Avenue—an avenue so bottlenecked with traffic around the Gansevoort marketplace and so plagued by frequent accidents involving trucks, trains, and trolleys that it had become known as Death Avenue. Vintage photographs of the meatpacking neighborhood before the High Line was built speak to rough-and-tumble days when food was brought by around four hundred horse-drawn wagons that choked the area and must have smelled unbearably fetid, especially since refrigeration was not installed in the Gansevoort market until 1904. Nearby and close to the piers lived longshoremen, teamsters, and meatpackers—types one could easily spot in Elia Kazan's *On the Waterfront*, filmed directly across the Hudson in New Jersey.

Today, the long, improbable hanging park that starts on Gansevoort Street and slithers all the way to West Thirty-Fourth Street still grazes the same tenements, the same old warehouses, rooftops, storage facilities, garages, and abandoned but refurbished factories that have mostly turned into affluent lofts. It still tunnels its way through the same buildings, unabashedly spying into private windows and offering stunning if sporadic vistas of the Hudson. The High Line bears all the features of urban art: part urban chic, part urban preservation, and part urban *reconquista*. The High Line has restored what seemed totally lost and foregone, and in the process brought out something totally unprecedented. The glam factor of the structure grows out of the exquisite symbiosis of grit with glitz.

You can almost touch the mingling of the two, for the High Line makes no secret of its inner-city origins. Indeed, it proclaims its rough, in-your-face, hardscrabble provenance like a child who was born in nineteenth-century working-class squalor but has finally risen to the top without ever caring for damask or table manners. The calluses show and are meant to show. For all the luxury surrounding the park today, it knows it wasn't born into anything remotely posh. The wild shrubs and the trees-of-heaven that had sprouted and were there before the makeover have been removed. Now, a long, flyover aluminum grating straddles the tufted large big-leaf magnolia trees that have the look of something that was there before the restorers had a hand in altering the flora. The still-unrestored section of the High Line that curves all the way west and then, Sloan-like, around Hudson Yards from Thirtieth to Thirty-Fourth streets gives a perfect picture of how feral the abandoned El must have looked and does still look. Much of the wild, spontaneous growth will be cut down or trimmed, but a pristine ailanthus arbor facing the Javits Center on Thirty-Fourth will be preserved, while a new, dazzling complex of buildings rise in this section of town now used as a train depot.

Walking along this unshorn section of the El I picked up a huge rusted nail. I scoured it, trying to clean it as best as I could. It will never look perfect. But it now sits on my desk as a paperweight.

THE HIGH LINE, WHICH WAS REFURBISHED and finally reopened in 2009, is a park that loves itself, its past, and its city. It has all the untamed, disheveled growth you expect to find on any abandoned railway track. The same goes for the tracks themselves. They are still there, and there is every attempt to remind the flâneur on today's High Line that this promenade is nothing more than a symbiotic medley of plants, tracks, and cement, and that the facelift has tried its best to leave things "as is" and not produce an Eliza Doolittle with bad wrinkles.

Yet the rails, which had suffered through decades of neglect but couldn't quite die or rot away, were not just left there and planted over. They were removed, cleansed of their asbestos, and only then put back in their original emplacements—the way the whole park, when you come to think of it, has been tamed and deloused without losing its self-seeded character. The park remembers its unshorn days of abandonment. But it isn't held hostage to them. And in this compromise lies art.

A walk through the park is a walk through a hodgepodge of incidentals that are intended to prolong the illusion of urban neglect without the rusty, infested, icky feel of neglect itself. The park is soigné without being manicured, unassuming without being slovenly. Nothing is left to chance. Not a seedling hasn't been fastidiously coddled; not a dimmed light isn't dimmed with purpose. Even the sounds are not unintended. This is the cynosure of staged spontaneity and staged abandonment; what the ever-incisive Restoration poet Robert Herrick, in an effort to describe that bewitching je ne sais quoi in a woman's manner of dress, once dubbed "wild civility." The Italians may have had a better word for it: *sprezzatura*—affected imperfection, willed neglect.

In all this there is something persistently spare and stark about the High Line that takes me back to those by-now almost-imaginary and half-remembered black-and-white images of Andreas Feininger, Berenice Abbott, and Eugene de Salignac. New York then, and New York now, what's lost, and what's restored, what's "as is" and what's airbrushed. Much as the passage of time changes and dates almost everything in those old photographs, some things remain constant. Every time I stare at an image of this or that aspect of the High Line in a photograph snapped in the last century and in one taken just a few hours ago, I stare at the differences and the similarities, knowing that looking at one picture without immediately turning to look at its far older cousin taken decades ago makes no sense, is insufficient, cheats time of its meaning. It is never clear to me whether it is permanence or change in these contrasting pairs of photographs that I wish to grasp. Chances are that the moment I decide it is change I am zeroing in on, I will instantly look for reassuring signs of permanence; but when I wish to see that nothing is altered, suddenly I'll spot all manner of differences that mark the passage of time. If there's a side of me that longs to live at the start of the twentieth century, another is grateful I'm alive in the twenty-first. If part of me loves the present, another yearns for an undefined time zone for which I still haven't given a name. Nineteen fifty-one, after all, is that arbitrary moment when John Sloan and I tagged each other before going our separate ways. These back-and-forth views are my way, and perhaps only mine, of trying to inhabit two zones, and in the process allot myself an extra margin of time, of life, an afterthought of meaning where finally, by miracle, I can finally see *other* and therefore *more* than what's just out there before me. On the High Line, and perhaps for a split second only, this is exactly what happens when I see the very old and the ultra-new at the same time, and, like Wordsworth craving to touch the invisible divide between France and Italy on the Simplon Pass in the Alps, I want to seize something he'd have called a spot of time.

It lasts, however, a very short while.

Whenever I near the High Line, my mind invariably drifts to a very good friend who lived on Horatio Street and whose guest I often was. I remember once hearing her tell me how she loved to walk along the river on West Street every afternoon and that her favorite moment occurred when the clock tower of the Erie Lackawanna Railroad and Ferry Terminal across the Hudson came into full view. She made plans to show me that exact spot along West Street, but we never took that walk together. Nor have I ever been to visit the restored terminal across the river—a project we both coddled, knowing that neither really wished to cross the Hudson. But I remember the view from her study, where we'd stare at the High Line in the days of its dereliction and never for a second think of what it would turn into in two decades. Staring at it from her window, she said it reminded her of elevated tracks in those black-and-white photographs of old New York and how, despite its ugliness and its clamor at night and the sheer bleakness of it, she understood John Sloan's romance with the Sixth Avenue El. She shared the romance of it herself, she said. I had never heard of John Sloan before. So she showed me his paintings in a book, saying that this painting in particular, *The City from Greenwich Village*, was one of the few things that made it possible for her to live with the High Line outside her window and never think it ugly at all. She was doing what I learned to do when I walk about the city these days and try to see more than what lies before me so that I can inject beauty and depth of meaning where ordinary experience confers so very little. We should take a walk under the High Line on our way to West Street, she said, and you'll see. But that walk was never to be. Had she been alive today she'd have loved nothing more than an afternoon walk all the way from Horatio to Thirty-Fourth Street and back. Now, when I'm in the neighborhood, I'll go up the stairs to the High Line, spot the window that was once hers, and think of her. Sometimes I still promise we'll walk together.

Hyde Park, London |
AMANDA FOREMAN

It came to me that Hyde Park has never belonged to London—
that it has always been, in spirit, a stretch of countryside; and that it
links the Londons of all periods together most magically—by
remaining forever unchanged at the heart of an ever-changing town.
—DODIE SMITH, *I Capture the Castle*, 1948

WHENEVER I ENTER HYDE PARK I am a child again, picking the rhododen-drons near Rotten Row. That is the first memory that assails me, no matter the time of year nor the purpose of my walk.

I remember straining to reach through the railings, each dew-flecked petal a sparkling gem that I yearned to possess. Occasionally, my fascina-tion with these crimson reds and royal violets proved stronger than my fear of the park police, and I would arrive home with my doll carriage overflow-ing with purloined flowers. But more usually I would walk along the rail-ings, aching with desire for the treasure within.

When it happened, I don't recall, but there came a time when the flow-ers in the park meant more than just unfulfilled longing. They awoke in me a consciousness and sense of comfort in life's rituals. The blooming of the daffodils and crocuses, followed by the tulips, and finally the rho-dodendrons and azaleas signaled the resumption of walks to the Lido for ice cream, cotton gingham dresses for afternoon games, and striped deck chairs on the meadow. Long before I could tell the hour or write the names of the months, the park existed as a living chronometer. Its springtime dis-play was proof that time passed but did not vanish. The flowers provided reassurance that memories were not only visions but also tethers to a pre-vious self that was not lost, simply changed. My little world had continuity and connection with the larger forces that ordered the ice cream and deck chairs to reappear each year.

For my grandmother, springtime in Hyde Park awoke some of her most vivid memories. Together we would amble beneath the elm trees, happy colluders in the filching of flowers, while she told me stories of London before the war. Back then, there was ice-skating on the Serpentine in the winter, and sheepdog trials in the summer. On Saturdays, Speaker's Corner was so busy that the crowds sometimes overflowed onto the road. On Sundays, it was the upper classes' turn to congregate, massing near the Knightsbridge barracks for the weekly "Church Parade" before lunch. The bombs changed all that. Though the rhododendrons were spared, the flower beds were turned into vegetable gardens. Nissen huts filled the lanes reserved riders and cyclists; giant searchlights and hulking artillery batteries occupied the meadow. There was no grass in those days, just a carpet of mud as far as the eye could see.

It seemed impossible to me, as I accompanied my grandmother on the deserted walk, that the Row was once the epicenter of fashionable London; or that the park could have thronged with people and riders, parading daily in a grand show of wealth and finery. If that was really true, I would ask her, where had they all gone? Where were the nannies she claimed to have seen, in their blue capes and starched uniforms with the little boys wearing sailor shorts even when it snowed? I don't remember ever having a satisfactory answer. The Row was still there, as was the Nannies Lawn, but their use had changed and the traditions associated with them were no longer practiced. Gradually it dawned on me that perhaps one day the customs of my childhood would fade away. There would be no Sunday ice creams at the Lido, just as there were no longer any fine ladies showing off their Ascot hats. Would the park remember? I thought not, and yet it seemed that the park itself was a repository of a vast collection of memories.

When we moved away from London, the rare sight of the park in bloom evinced a special sort of pain: the display had continued without me. Indeed everything continued as it was before. The ribbons of color that blaze through the park in springtime had not changed their hue nor altered their patterns just because I could not be present to enjoy them. A brisk morning in April still brought out the runners, the strollers, and the idlers, their jerky silhouettes enhanced by the acid pinks and oranges of the azaleas. Children walking home at teatime still scavenged for conkers and flowers. The plane trees lining the Broad Walk still glowed a golden yellow in the early evening twilight. I had joined the mass of nameless strangers who leave no trace upon the park, though it had surely left its trace on us. The trees endure; the gates stand; but I now understood that the figures basking in the sun or scurrying in the rain are ephemeral. This was the last and most enduring lesson I learned from the park during my childhood.

As I grew into adolescence, I developed an abundance of cynicism and suddenly Hyde Park became a place for children and old people. A teenager has no need to escape the roar of the city or to seek solace in nature's calm embrace. The Serpentine was dull, the flowers were dull, and dullest of all were the monuments and figures that adorned the park. Rather than seeing them as stone teardrops on the landscape, I thought they were vain exercises in futility. It came as a great surprise years later to discover that adulthood is not the end of the horizon but rather the beginning.

An even greater surprise, however, was the realization that the moral landscape of our existence is consciously echoed in the physical landscape of our daily lives. The style of these manifestations may shift and change according to the taste of each succeeding generation, but the motivations remain the same. When I did finally revisit Hyde Park in my twenties, unconsciously drawn to my childhood haunt near the Row, the path I happened to take led me to the Holocaust memorial, situated near the Dell, to the east of the Serpentine. It is not a bronze statue or a stone monument, but a small grove of silver birches surrounding two large boulders placed together with three smaller ones set apart on an irregular gravel bed. A bed of evergreens and shade-loving perennials separates the gravel from the trees, casting a pale green light on days when the sun filters through the branches. On that particular day, the morning's rain had left dark rivulets of tears on the sides of the largest boulder, framing the quotation from Lamentations engraved on the front. "For these I weep. Streams of tears flow from my eyes because of the destruction of my people."

Unaware of the Holocaust memorial until then, I was transfixed by the dignified beauty of the grove. My youthful cynicism had blinded me to the ways in which a park, especially Hyde Park, is a natural palimpsest for civic memory. I had never looked beyond the carved mottoes and grim-faced statues representing "Peace" and other such worthy aims, to consider what role these monuments played in shaping our responses to the past. But the Holocaust memorial was unlike anything I had ever seen. Modest and contained, it asks the visitor to reflect instead of demanding that she or he listen. There are no architectural allusions to mythic heroes or elaborate paeans to honor and sacrifice. The area is enclosed by the birch trees, but not cut off from the ordinary life of the park. It does not try to compete with its surroundings for attention. There is no guardrail or plinth that separates the boulders from the world. They simply exist in their own physical space. Yet I saw that the memorial answered a need in our collective consciousness to find expression when words alone cannot fulfill the task.

A few years after my first encounter with the Holocaust memorial, work began on a garden whose borders stretched from the tip of Hyde Park Corner almost to the edge of the memorial's outer perimeters. It was going to be a traditional rose garden, framed by pleached lime trees and double pergolas of rambling roses. My first and only thought was whether the new garden would encroach upon the memorial. Even though I could not claim the Holocaust memorial as a childhood memory, it felt to me as though it had always been there. Like the rhododendrons in springtime, the birch grove had its rhythms and associated rituals. The shadows lengthened and shortened according to the season; the gravel disappeared beneath a carpet of leaves in the autumn; the birch trees revealed their stark beauty in the winter. In my mind's eye, there was a seamless link between inspecting the flowers with my grandmother and bending down to read the inscriptions on the boulder.

When a landscape becomes an indelible part of our identity, it can feel as though any change, no matter how small, is a threat to the present we know and the past we have constructed. I loved Hyde Park precisely because it had managed to remain unchanged even though, like the sea, its natural state is one of constant renewal. Far from dismissing the park's landmarks and monuments as I once had, as an adult I found solace in their timeless meditations on living and loss. Without having seen the relationship between the new Rose Garden and the Holocaust memorial, I had assumed that the delicate balance between the park and the little grove would not survive the arrival of its showier neighbor. It did not occur to me that a new dialogue might emerge from the altered landscape, one that engaged different, but equally, profound sentiments and sensibilities.

The entrance to the Rose Garden from the direction of the Holocaust memorial is through one of its several pergola walks. The path unfolds in a gentle curve beneath a shroud of scented blossoms. So knotted are the trailing vines that only brief glimpses of the park beyond are allowed to shine through. Simply walking into the tunnel is an act of surrender and belief: it requires an acceptance that behind lies one form of reality, while another waits ahead. For lovers of children's literature, the rose tunnel is homage to the looking glass, the first star on the right, the wardrobe, and the brass knob at the end of the bed.

Inside the garden lies a sequence of spaces or open rooms in the classic English tradition. With every step, the scent of lavender and Russian sage intermingles with the heavy perfume of old English roses. A winding path leads to a circular border of climbing roses on chain swags—a favorite planting scheme of the Edwardians—enclosing an inner garden of muted pink perennials and white roses surrounding the famous *Boy and Dolphin* fountain by Alexander Munro. Here, water flows from the dolphin's nostrils, recalling its previous incarnation as the largest and most important provider of fresh drinking water in the park.

In contrast to the silent void at the heart of the Holocaust memorial, where tranquility is equated with the absence of human presence, the Rose Garden offers the possibility of Arcadia wrought anew, not by divine, but by human intervention. Rather than coexisting as independent satellites, as I had feared, they serve as the perfect counterweights to one another. Nowadays, I will always combine a visit to the memorial with a walk through the garden. I come because of the pleasure I feel in remembering. My childhood memories rise to the surface and become imbued with the sensations of the present. But I am also drawn to these gardens because they tell a story of people and events that have no other way of being shared. The two together, the garden of life and the memorial of death, more any other landmark or feature of Hyde Park, fill me with hope that the past is never truly beyond the bounds of our imagination.

Iveagh Gardens, Dublin |
JOHN BANVILLE

LOVE AMONG THE LEAVES

I FIRST SAW PARIS WHEN I WAS EIGHTEEN. It was a good age to experience a momentous epiphany. At eighteen one is grown-up enough not to be overly alarmed by the great world's wonders, yet young enough to register them with fresh-eyed openness. When I say I *saw* Paris I mean it literally, for I spent almost all of my time there out of doors. The shabby little hotel on the Rue Molière where I rented a fifth-floor *chambre de bonne* discouraged guests from hanging about the place during the daytime, and I could not afford long restaurant lunches or to lounge for hours in Left Bank cafés. And so I walked and looked, and looked and walked.

What impressed me at once were the statues. In Ireland we tend to erect tremendous plinths and set upon them tiny figurines, our aspirations to *gloire* seeming to diminish at an ascending rate. In Paris, however, vast stone figures stride toward us imperiously, overwhelming in their scale, their grandeur, their vividness. From that long-ago visit I recall in particular venturing into the Jardin du Luxembourg for the first time. It was a September afternoon, the great trees dappled with sunlight the color of straw and a hazing of fine blond dust adrift in the air. Watching the bourgeoisie in its self-conscious promenade, the dreamily strolling lovers, the children at play, I felt as though I had stepped into a painting by Renoir or Raoul Dufy.

Years later I sometimes stayed in a friend's apartment near the Luxembourg Gardens, and would take my daughter there in the afternoons. She was a toddler and delighted in the place. Now and then she would halt in front of one of those great statues and peer up at it with a mixture of awe and inquiry, as if the figure had spoken to her. Now she is grown-up and living in Paris, and the Luxembourg is one of her favorite haunts.

WE HAVE BEEN ACCUSTOMED TO THEM for so long that we forget what a remarkable invention parks and pleasure gardens are. Although they are as old as antiquity—think of the Hanging Gardens of Babylon—parks are the quintessential public work of the Enlightenment, especially in England and, by extension, America. While Andrew Marvell wrote not only "The Garden" but also "The Mower Against Gardens," Alexander Pope saw the polite cultivation of sward and hedge as fit work for a species bent on achieving its apotheosis by way of control and bounded elegance. Brute nature must be tamed in the cause of good manners. The park maker's aim is to soothe and civilize. Manhattan's Central Park is surely the most expensive tract of real estate ever given over to the pursuit of leisure.

Grandeur, however, is all very well, but I suspect each one of us has some more modest, secret place in which to wander and delight. In the early 1960s, when I left the small Irish town where I was born and came to live in Dublin, I found that I gravitated most frequently toward the city's parks; nostalgia, perhaps, for my rural roots. There was the Phoenix Park, of course, that great sprawling semi-wilderness that runs for miles beside the Liffey—the largest walled park in Europe, it is said—but somehow I never felt at home there, or perhaps on the contrary, I felt too much at home, recalling the fields and wooded slopes surrounding my hometown. St. Stephen's Green, in the Georgian heart of Dublin, on the other hand, has its suave charms such that Pope would have approved, but in its altogether too-well-barbered stateliness seemed to me deserving of Marvell's mower's frowning complaint that

> *'Tis all enforced, the fountain and the grot,*
> *While the sweet fields do lie forgot*

THE IVEAGH GARDENS, not far from St. Stephen's Green, are modest, not richly appointed, and wear an air of faint melancholy. They suit me, though, and of all the parks in Dublin I like them best. I was already in my forties when I discovered them, quite late. In fact, I should not say *discovered*, since I am sure I would never have found them by myself. I was introduced to the grounds by a girl whom at the time I was busy falling in love with— fruitlessly, as it would turn out. She was already spoken for, and our trysts, few as they were, had to take place well away from the public gaze of Dublin, one of the world's most vigilantly prurient cities.

There was a secret place, she told me, that almost no one knew about. We went there for the first time on a hurried but never-to-be-forgotten lunch hour; she brought sandwiches and I, hopefully, a bottle of wine that in the end turned out not to have the desired seductive effect. It was early autumn, and under a Poussin sky the trees were that dry-olive shade that they take on before the final turn, and made a wistful, dreamy rustling high above us in the pale blue air. Before we settled to our picnic she insisted on showing me around what she seemed to consider her private domain. I see us there, clear as day and as if it were yesterday, pacing the gravel paths beside the pleasingly unkempt lawns, under those restive trees. Here are the fountains, there is the archery range—and oh, smell that fragrance wafting from the rose garden over the way! Supposedly there was a maze, too, she said, but she had never been able to find it. I held her hand. It was hopeless, she said, hopeless, and yet she smiled and let her hand rest in mine. It is out of such moments, commonplace yet plangent, that places take on their significance.

The gardens, naturally, have their own past. They are first mentioned publicly in the mid-eighteenth century as Leeson's Fields. The land was leased to a developer by the name of Hatch, who used it as the garden of a house on Harcourt Street built for the attorney general, Lord Clonmell, an enthusiastic toper who was quaintly and no doubt accurately known as Copperfaced Jack. In 1810 Clonmell House was sold and the space behind it was opened to the public as Coburg Gardens. In the early 1860s the site was purchased by Benjamin Guinness, scion of the brewing family. Benjamin, like so many of the Guinness family then and now, was of a philanthropic cast, and he seems to have lent or perhaps leased the land to the splendidly named Dublin Exhibition Palace and Winter Garden Company, to be the pleasure grounds of the Dublin International Exhibition, held in 1865.

The Exhibition Building, which would in time become University College Dublin—and the core of which survives today as part of the National Concert Hall—was a very grand affair, with an adjoining Winter Garden, a vaulted hall of glass and steel the structural stability of which was tested by "monitoring hundreds of running workmen, 600 marching men of the 78th Highlanders and the rolling of several thousand cannonballs." (This gem of trivial information I glean from *Dublin*, by the art historian Christine Casey; it is the first and, so far as I know, only volume in the Buildings of Ireland series from Yale University Press, and is greatly to be recommended.)

Meanwhile Benjamin Guinness had purchased Nos. 78–81 on St. Stephen's Green and combined them into a fine mansion, Iveagh House—now home of the Irish Department of Foreign Affairs—and with the exhibition over, reclaimed the gardens and commissioned the landscape architect Ninian Niven—how resonant the names were in those days!—to

164

furnish a new design, combining French and English landscaping styles. In 1908 Benjamin Guinness's son Edward, first Earl of Iveagh, donated the gardens to University College, which in Edward's honor renamed them Iveagh Gardens.

By the time I came to them, the gardens, now backing both the National Concert Hall and the Department of Foreign Affairs, had fallen again into happy neglect.

They are not large, being I imagine about the size of a football field. Features include, so the guidebooks tell me, rustic grottoes and a cascade, two fountains, woodlands and a wilderness, a rosarium, an American garden, archery grounds, rockeries and rooteries—not quite sure what these last-named are—and a maze. The maze in particular pleases me, since in all the times I have visited the gardens, I, like that long-ago lost girl of mine, have never succeeded in finding it. It is one thing to be astray in a maze, but that there should be a maze one cannot find strikes me as a truly marvelous thing, a fancy straight out of a tale by Borges. I often entertain the notion that if there were to be an afterlife, there would be worse ways of enduring it than in an endless Borgesian circular search for this mystery garden within gardens.

In the mid-1990s the Office of Public Works instituted a renovation of the Iveagh Gardens. Good work was done, I suppose, but I preferred them in their prelapsarian dishevelment of the old days, when I went wistfully courting there. Parks—and let us grant that this little plot can aspire to the condition of a park—are mysterious, indeed at times sinister, places. Remember Antonioni's *Blow-Up*? Who having seen that film will forget the agitated soughing of trees on the soundtrack while David Hemmings's fashion photographer is developing a roll of snapshots taken in a London park and discovering that he has captured on film what seems to be the commission of a murder? Certain habitués of parks seem to be *up to something*. One can come upon a figure huddled on the grass, eyes shut, cheek on hand, clothing all awry, and walk on with the uneasy question in one's mind: was he sleeping, or . . . ? This faint hint of pervading menace is part of the pleasure of parks for me, just as much as the fountains and the flower beds.

And then there are the statues. I am sorry to say that there is a great paucity of them in Iveagh Gardens. The twin fountains are manned by a facing pair of identical, muscular angels with disproportionately large hands—for holding up the righteous out of the clutches of the forces of evil?—and on concrete plinths there stand a few vague, less-than-life-size female figures, all of them noseless, their complexions marred by lichen, gazing downward in weariness and seeming dejection. "An account of 1872 described figures of the Spirits of the Land, a figure of Erin seated on shamrocks, figures of the Four Provinces and of St Patrick." Hmm. Somehow I do not feel compelled to mourn the passing of these paragons. A modern figure cast in muddy bronze of the tenor John McCormack stands in a holly bower, mouth agape like that of a baby bird demanding to be fed. He looks so sad, giving his mute all to the unheeding greenery roundabout. But then, he would not be happy, either, I suspect, in the Jardin du Luxembourg, dwarfed by the figures of so many of his heroic confrères.

MY MOST RECENT VISIT to the Iveagh Gardens was in the company of my younger daughter. She is sixteen. I have brought her with me to show her a place precious to me, where I was once sweetly unhappy in love. I discover, to my great surprise, that she knows the place well. Her boyfriend, it turns out, lives nearby, and it is here, on weekdays after school, that they come to walk, and be together, discussing the great issues of the day, finding out about each other, learning to grow up. As she tells me this, in her offhand way, I have a sense of the magical timelessness of such places, and of the uses to which we put them. We change, we age, we stay or move away, and in time we end. The park, however, endures. It is a thought, I think, to comfort the most distressed of hearts.

Jardin du Luxembourg, Paris |
AMANDA HARLECH

GHOST LOVE

THE LUXEMBOURG GARDEN is not a garden, nor is it a municipal park, but like a paradigm of Paris, it is both highly artificial and as natural as children playing hide-and-seek in an orchard. It is not what I'd expected when I arrived in Paris as a belligerently sentimental twenty-year-old, still up at Oxford and polishing off a Grand Tour of European churches and galleries with a brilliant but tricky historian called Pierre. I was in love with him, an unregulated obsession that sprang up in that spring of 1979. But it was unrequited. I trailed after him through the dank frankincense of Byzantine churches, nursing little hooks in my heart—a heart that had been fed Wyatt, James, and Rilke—dragging my leather suitcase much like the baggage of my desire. I was unprepared to let go even if I secretly questioned Pierre's grandiose dismissal of rucksacks, sneakers, and shortcuts.

We had returned hungry and penniless to stay with his mother in her leafy, book-lined apartment on the Boulevard Raspail. But there was to be no release from Pierre's mise-en-scène—his Gallic pride transformed him into a stylish Belmondo, glamorous delinquency replacing the gritty Yorkshire determination of the last few weeks—and I, ever the devoted acolyte, was now cast as a femme fatale in his moody film noir, starring doomed youth in Paris. Pierre's way of expressing the violence of his romantic impasse was to draw up dramatic and visually intricate schedules for our opening act. This was not like my trip to the Louvre when I was eleven, with a dandified, alcoholic godfather, nor was it like the family car journey back from our farmhouse in Spain when we fell out of the dusty Volvo, brown and feral and impatient to eat croque monsieur and frites at the Flore before making the ferry and the night trip back to England and the autumn term. Pierre was a pathfinder, a diviner of the truth of a place. He had the eye of a nineteenth-century novelist with a sense for that rare strangeness in obscure detail.

He was adamant that I should feel Paris—listen to this wise, well-preserved courtesan as well as watch her. There is far more to Paris than meets the eye. She is a city of elegance, violence, perfume, philosophical significance, ritual, and fishwives. She is arch, vain, polished, and highly strung. Paris is the Queen of Fashion and the seducer of Time.

Pierre woke me in the morning with a rap on my door. The historian's voice-over had been switched off. He stood in silence, staring at me provocatively before throwing his blue and white T-shirt and a Breton fishing sweater at my head. I guessed they were for me to wear and hoped this costume change had been triggered by a change of heart. Maybe the collar of his tweed jacket would no longer be turned up against some unguarded tenderness. He took me for a breakfast of café au lait and tartines in the Coupole, reading *Le Monde* like a windsurfer in a gale, the newspaper sails fixed to wooden poles. He bought me Gitanes Maïs—impossible to smoke but authentic, he told me, laughing as the loosely packed tobacco stuck to my lip through the damp maize paper.

It was a bright May morning and the breeze was warm and freighted with the narcotic of lime blossom, lilac, and hyacinth. Why do the florist shops look like confectioners, I asked, beaming with a new bravery. Because Paris prides herself on her civilizing power over nature, like makeup, silk, and lace, he replied, pulling up the collar of his scratchy Hebden tweed. I suspected I was missing the point. We were walking up the Rue de Fleurus to the sound of running water. Paris is the city of transformation. As with any ritual that appeared random—the language of fans, or kissing someone you barely knew on both cheeks—I was fascinated by the secret logic of miniature dams made of floor cloths and rags angled in gutters to divert the water sluice and by the covert process by which they had come to be so carefully placed, morning after morning, season after season.

Paris, with her architectural clarity, her classical proportions, her thoughtful radius of boulevards, had me under her spell. Unlike the medieval confusion of London circumnavigated by ponderous old father Thames, everything in Paris shone in the reflected light of the Seine beneath wide, uncluttered skies. Where are you taking me? Le Jardin du Luxembourg—there isn't another garden like it in the world. Not Kensington Gardens or Central Park. It is a sanctuary in a city orchestrated around Marie de' Medici's childhood garden at the Pitti Palace in Florence. It is my secret garden, Pierre replied so softly I thought he was speaking to an elsewhere, a memory of somebody, or himself maybe.

I had been brought up to understand that Parisian public gardens were places where you couldn't walk on the grass, with sculpted yews and pollarded allées of chestnut trees. They were like the court of Versailles, demonstrations of the power of civilizing intelligence and wealth. Parterres embroidered like lace handkerchiefs, decorated with fountains and statues like jewelry. But the idea of a garden that had been created to reproduce a child's sense of home—and maybe this is what we really mean by "love"—begged from the Duc de Luxembourg as a refuge after the assassination of Henri IV—seemed to me the epitome of the garden as a paradise, an Eden within a protective wall. Marie de' Medici must have been drawn to the solace of the Carthusian monastery of the original garden with the seasonal rhythm of the *pépinière* orchards and vineyards. She would have wanted relief from the humiliation and intrigue of the court, of her own sons' vicious, murderous intentions, and to escape from her own blind fecklessness. Even if, as we turned off the Rue de Vaugirard, and walked up the wide gravel path between the careful lines of pollarded trees, the garden seemed as formal as the ancient courtoisie of French medieval romance, there were people here, quietly content with whatever they were doing—rather in the way the Carthusian monks would have tended their orchard of espaliered apples and pears, which still provides chartreuse for the Senate. There is a sense that time has been stopped in the Jardin du Luxembourg. Where the white elephant of Rilke's poem ("Le Carrousel, Jardin du Luxembourg," 1905) still follows the lion and the deer and the spotted carousel prancing horses, where children still sail boats on the octagonal pond, where students congregate in smoky knots by the St. Michel gate, and where chess players and ancients sit beneath the chestnut trees.

We sat on a bench. For a few moments we forgot ourselves, and we had become the foreground of a nineteenth-century Seeberger brothers photograph: the stipple of the leaves, the skim and scream of a pair of swifts, low across the basin, the three children in their school pinafores eating ice-cream cones and dragging a puppy up the steps to a balustrade brandishing a pair of vast Nubian stone lions who appeared oddly cruel as if another life stood just out of reach in the ink of their shadows. A mother called out to a pair of blond boys throwing sand at each other, while in the lull of stone and leaf and fountain, a band began to play. I felt as if this world, unfolding in the drowse of heat, was something that I'd known before, something that would continue to gather and scatter in its own rhythm forever. An old woman stood at the edge of the pool. A single black feather in her hat ducked and fretted in the breeze. She seemed to be searching for something below the surface of the water as though she had lost a ring and was hoping to catch a moment's magnification of gold among the dark green weed. She bent down abruptly, rummaging in the bag at her feet before straightening and casting a spell of bread crumbs for the ducks and the carp. I realized that Pierre was showing me a snapshot of his childhood in Paris.

I have never forgotten that morning in May in the Jardin du Luxembourg. Often when I'm staying in Paris I will retrace that walk and stand, lost in every passing moment of the past, in the beat of the present—in the rain, in the magnification of snow, in early spring when the orange trees and palms are brought out and unwrapped from their winter cladding, or in the blinding blue of July—and sense the haunting of first love in Paris. Ghosts of ourselves, of all who went before, watch from the bend in the path as it turns beyond the foliage. There is laughter and a sudden dart of movement in the shadow of the statue of George Sand; a ball is thrown from nowhere and rolls to a stop in front of the apiary. Only the bees continue working away at this old story that is retold for everyone who stands and watches and listens in the Jardin du Luxembourg.

Lincoln Park and Grant Park,
Chicago |

JONATHAN ALTER

ALEXANDER HAMILTON WAS A MERE STATUE across the street, not a park. He wasn't Abraham Lincoln or even Ulysses S. Grant, who had the distinct advantage in my five-year-old mind of being presidents of the United States. Lincoln and Grant, sixteenth and eighteenth in the pantheon respectively, got whole places named for them. Hamilton, the cleverest founder, didn't make the cut. I knew this fact, knew it cold, because I learned to say—or more precisely, sing—thirty-five presidents in a row right through John F. Kennedy in 1962. It was a party favor proffered by my parents to friends and relatives after the second or third martini in exchange for a few loving laughs. Bring Jonny out in his feet pajamas to recite all the presidents as fast as he could—first name, middle initial, last name—with a hammy pride that remains undiminished, I'm embarrassed to say, in the half century since. "The world's only historian who can't read!" my father would proudly exclaim.

We lived just by Lincoln Park, which runs up and down the North Side along the shores of Lake Michigan. Grant Park, sometimes known as the front yard of downtown Chicago, lies a few miles south, also along the lakefront. When I was little, the park represented the larger world outside my window. I couldn't yet cross Lakeview Avenue by myself to enter Lincoln Park, much less wander east toward the lake. My sister had tried to do so when she was six, later claiming that she had held her own hand. This didn't fly with the policeman who escorted her home, or with my parents. To reach the Hamilton statue near Wrightwood and the mammoth marble walkway (long since removed) beneath it, I was compelled to extend my tiny paw out of my snow jacket into the Chicago frost. At least one of the mittens my mother had attached several times to the cuff with a toothed metal snap was long gone, which meant that I would need to hold hands bare with Mom or Dad or Helga or Mrs. Brennan or one of the other housekeepers I can't remember, not just across the street and past the Hamilton statue but through a dark stone tunnel (that seems much smaller now) to the Lincoln Park Lagoon, where the swings made me nauseous.

At least my snug world was expanding from the apartment and kindergarten and grandparents to the wonders of Lincoln Park, where I could watch chicks hatch at the zoo and always find a balloon somewhere. Mom wanted me and my three siblings to appreciate the weeping willows and the bird sanctuary. Dad took us sledding on Devil's Hill and later, when we moved farther north, to Hawthorne Place, to see the huge totem pole near Addison, just four blocks east of Wrigley Field. We played tennis and ice-skated at Waveland Avenue, where the wind whipped right in from the lake. No one quite knows how Chicago came to be called the "Windy City," though historians (who read) now believe it was less about weather than the long-winded politicians of the nineteenth century.

American history continued to be a part of my personal history. Well into my grade school years, mom still baked me a cake every February 12 on Lincoln's birthday, though I wouldn't dare admit it to my friends. We were besotted with sports now, strutting toward the park before dark for some tackle football without pads in the fall or Chicago-style sixteen-inch softball (no mitts allowed) in the spring. On scorching days, we'd be too lazy to find the beach at Fullerton or Oak Street and just swim off the rocks. A dangerous pastime. Every excursion was also a real-life education, with early exposure to bikini-clad Polish or Lithuanian or Ukrainian or Irish or some other kind of girls from wards that were different than our own. It was fun to check out the oddballs who have always found refuge in parks, some homeless (though we didn't use the word then), some just anxious for attention. Refreshment consisted of holding down the waterspouts on the park's rough-hewn stone fountains so that water would spurt into the face of the other kid trying to get a drink.

One winter day in sixth grade I called my friend Casey and asked if he wanted to go play hockey in the park. He said he couldn't because his mother had died after surgery. His father had died of cancer when we were in fourth grade and he and his little brother, Barnaby, had no other relatives who would raise them. A family from our school that they barely knew had agreed to take them in. After the funeral, the mourners went back to their house on Wrightwood, while Casey and Barnaby slipped out and went to Lincoln Park. There they played catch—baseball and football, out of season—until they dropped. Years later, Casey told me of the restorative powers of the park that day, how it was only then, not far from the statue of the half-naked poet Goethe (pronounced "Go-Thee" by Chicago cabdrivers), that the brothers knew everything would somehow be okay.

That August, the bus from camp deposited me at the Conrad Hilton Hotel, across Michigan Avenue from Grant Park. Two weeks later, I was back at the mammoth Hilton, the host hotel for the 1968 Democratic National Convention, already racked by confrontations between "longhairs" protesting the Vietnam War and Mayor Richard J. Daley's police. My mother was working for Hubert Humphrey and my father for Eugene McCarthy and I was underfoot in both headquarters, inhaling an historic convention at close range. One day someone threw a stink bomb into the lobby. I can smell it still. The newspapers ran a picture of the cops tossing a demonstrator and his bike into the Lincoln Park Lagoon. Near the Grant Park bandshell, Abbie Hoffman's comical Youth International Party, the Yippies, nominated a pig for president.

Before I knew what was happening, my mother grabbed my ten-year-old hand, harder than on Lakeview, the danger eclipsing any embarrassment. By the time we got the car from the parking lot, Michigan Avenue in front of the Hilton was lined with police, poised to club kids, reporters, anyone who got in the way. Soon a "police riot," as a commission later called it, was under way. An activist we knew named Don Rose began a chant: "The whole world is watching! The whole world is watching!" And it was. The old Democratic Party died in Grant Park that night, ensuring the election of Richard Nixon that year and fueling the new conservative ascendancy. At home, "Lakefront Liberals," Chicago's proto-yuppies, pushed back, and in the aftermath of the convention some made it to public office, including my mom, the first woman elected in Cook County.

Around this time, Dad began using the scenic bike path along the lakefront, not just on weekends, but to commute ten miles to his office on the South Side, an eccentricity then that would pass unnoticed today. In Grant Park, he turned his trusty ten-speed west toward the Conrad Hilton at Balbo Street, named for Mussolini's fascist air marshal, Italo Balbo, who caused a sensation when he led twenty-four silver seaplanes to land in Lake Michigan as part of Chicago's 1933 "Century of Progress" World's Fair. Today there is growing sentiment to strip the Nazi-loving thug of his place of honor and rename Balbo for another, much worthier man of Italian descent, Ron Santo, the beloved third baseman and announcer for the Chicago Cubs.

As I grew older, I took it for granted that my hometown allowed me to catch a Cubs game at Wrigley Field and hit the Oak Street beach in the same afternoon. I could play tennis and skeet-shoot, too, at least in theory. Riding past a now-defunct lakefront rifle range on my bike, I could smell the shells and imagine myself on a firing line in World War II, the imaginary game of choice for boys of my generation. But this part of the public park wasn't public at all. Later I wondered how certain privileged adults could day after day monopolize the supposedly public courts of the Lincoln Park Tennis Club and use the Lincoln Park Gun Club to heedlessly pollute the lake with what I later learned was 2,700 metric tons of lead. And of course their boats got all the available slips in the harbors.

The answer was that they had clout. Like everything else in Chicago, the parks were run under the old Daley Machine as a patronage fiefdom. The great bard of Chicago, the late columnist Mike Royko, wrote in 1966 that the motto emblazoned on the seal of the city, *Urbs in Horto*—Latin for "City in a Garden"—should be changed to *Ubi Est Mea* ("Where's Mine?"). The Park District boss in late midcentury was Ed Kelly, whose infamous no-bid contracts to concessionaires rendered all park food inedible except, to my young palate, the buttery caramel corn. Interlopers were unwelcome, especially when crime went up. In the 1960s, Daley and Kelly were so afraid of black muggers that they ordered many of the bushes removed from Lincoln Park.

Chicago has always been racially polarized. In 1919, a small group of black kids drifted in the water over an invisible line to a white beach. Angry whites stoned them and a major race riot left dozens dead and hundreds injured. Even now, de facto segregation cleaves the city. Minorities are mostly confined to beautifully designed but erratically maintained parks that lie miles to the west of the lake. The long line of high-rises across Lake Shore Drive from the beach make for a gleaming steel curtain breached only occasionally and at the risk of cultural conflict. For years, Latino groups proposed that the Park District mark off soccer fields in the city's parks. But Kelly decreed that the American game was football and any soccer goals must be fashioned from football uprights. This was life in another century, though even today Chicagoans rarely pause to admit that the beach volleyball and kayaking and pedicab riding in the lakefront parks are still mostly the recreational activities of whites.

But the politicians must have done something right. Moving around as an adult, I noticed something obvious—that New York and Los Angeles lay adjacent to oceans but don't have beaches downtown. Neither do other Great Lakes cities like Cleveland and Milwaukee, where industry has despoiled much of the lakefront. It wasn't until I got to Miami and Honolulu that I saw beaches in the shadow of American skyscrapers.

By now I can read history, of course, and I learned that the impulse to protect Chicago's "front yard" began even before the city was incorporated. In 1836, Congress granted Illinois land to open a canal connecting the Illinois River to Lake Michigan. The new Canal Commission decreed that the lakefront should be "Public Ground—Common to Remain Open, Clear and Free of any Buildings or Other Obstructions Whatever." During the Civil War, the area that was to become Lincoln Park was used as a burial ground for soldiers, including Confederate prisoners, later joined by victims of the 1871 Chicago Fire. Grant Park was partly a train depot. I learned all about Chicago's greatest visionary, Daniel Burnham, who in 1909 offered a master plan for the city that was most notable for what it didn't do—develop the lakefront. Instead, the Burnham Plan made sure the lakefront stayed open, clear, and free. "Make no little plans," Burnham wrote. "They have not the power to stir men's souls."

As we were growing up, these words were not the dusty pronouncements of a long-dead architect but a worthy (if grandiose) blueprint for our own lives, limned in our family DNA. In the 1980s, my father led a civic group called "Friends of the Parks," which holds the Park District accountable to the public. Now, at ninety, from his retirement apartment overlooking Belmont Harbor, he reminds me that more city dwellers use parks on a regular basis than they do police, fire, or any other local service. Parks are stitched into their lives, often on a daily basis. That means fevered public debate over even seemingly minor matters, like where to put a flower bed, or which sections can be closed off for special events. In 1981 and again in 2012, promoters tried to turn the Grant Park into a racetrack, with plans for a Formula One and later an IndyCar Chicago Grand Prix race. The public, determined to relax undisturbed by checkered flags, said no.

But other big changes have been spectacularly well received. In 2004, under prodding from Mayor Richard M. Daley, the city opened Millennium Park on 24.5 acres of northwest Grant Park, a shimmering green roof over some old railroad tracks and parking lots. Despite the city's other problems, the half-billion-dollar public-private partnership has put a welcome gloss on downtown Chicago. The centerpiece is the Pritzker Pavilion, the Frank Gehry–designed outdoor performance center that now hosts Lollapalooza and other music festivals. Taste of Chicago, which has grown since 1980 to be the world's largest food festival, has drawn as many as three and a half million people to the area.

But nothing in the history of Grant Park can compare to what happened on November 4, 2008. I was in an emotionally wrought state, though not for the reasons of the hundreds of thousands who gathered on an unseasonably warm evening, without a single arrest, to witness the victory speech of America's first black president. My mother, who knew Barack Obama from his days as a community organizer, would be dead within a week. Her spirit was already with me in the park as the president-elect began his address before the world: "If there is anyone out there who still doubts that America is a place where all things are possible; who still wonders if the dream of our founders is alive in our time; who still questions the power of our democracy, tonight is your answer." Within minutes he was quoting Lincoln in Grant Park.

We were standing only twenty blocks from where the 1919 race riots began and on the very spot where the 1968 convention disturbances brought bitterness to American politics. Now, for at least this night, Chicago's tortured racial history receded. Retired cops, retired hippies, and their descendants gathered in pride, this time on the same side of the barricades. In the years ahead, some hopes were dashed on the rocks of partisan politics, but that night in Grant Park would be lodged forever in our memories, and in the consciousness of the world.

The president was in the park. Amid the throngs, I felt dazed and transported. I was in a beautiful green space, in the middle of a great American city, touching humanity, history, and home.

The Maidan, Calcutta | SIMON WINCHESTER

PERHAPS IT WOULD BE MOST SUITABLE to begin this story with my first sighting of the Maidan, the old parade ground that is now Calcutta's largest public park. Conventionally, that first sight should have been the most romantic—before some long-ago sunrise, as I was walking barefoot across the dew-damp grass onto the cool marble of the Victoria Memorial, yearning for a moment's peace before the morning mayhem of India's most bewilderingly crowded city. Or perhaps it should have been at some sunset, as I was gazing westward over the grasslands while sipping pink gin in a tea merchant's comfortable mansion on Chowringhee.

But that's not what happened. In fact, my first real memory of the Maidan is stranger and very different. It relates to a curious chapter of accidents, which began one hot summer's afternoon when I spied a ladder propped up against the high walls of Fort William, the monumental, British-built Indian army castle that stands in the Maidan's center. I suddenly knew beyond a shadow of doubt that the ladder's wooden steps were made for climbing—by me.

I realize some context might be useful: The Maidan owes its very existence to Fort William. Its fourteen hundred acres of well-trimmed greenery—or what was once greenery; this being India, it is now a sort of unkempt brownery—once served a purely military need. When the eighteenth-century imperialists built their great fort, they were so nervous of attack from wily locals that they created a huge clear field of fire entirely around it. The fort remains today—never once having been attacked, nor ever used even once to fire down on anyone—as does the field of fire, a space designed first and foremost as a place where no enemy could ever hide. So the grassland that Calcutta treasures today, the one great emptiness where its citizens can breathe some semblance of fresh air, came not as the result of planning for a pleasaunce or a strolling ground or a home for offerings of flower beds; it was designed not to be poked about with parasols, or walked over in stilettos, but in extremis to be raked by hails of bullets from London-made Maxim guns.

It was also for purely military reasons that I decided to step up onto that oh-so-tempting wooden ladder. For there was a famous old building inside the walls that I had long wanted to photograph. At the time I was writing a book about Britain's architectural legacy in India, along with Jan Morris, and we both knew that inside Fort William were some priceless gems. Especially this one structure in particular.

But these days the Indian army steadfastly forbids all civilians entrance to Fort William. Especially foreigners. And most especially Britons, as former colonialists. It was an order I should have abided, except that on this happy day in Calcutta, when all I had been doing was strolling through the Maidan looking for memorable pictures to take, here was this ladder, with twenty short and easy steps. It was a sign. And once I had managed to get myself inside the fort, I consoled myself: What could anyone do, except throw me out, along with my pictures? Punishment couldn't be much worse than that, surely?

So I asked Hassan, my driver, to wait beside the car and say nothing. Glancing around quickly to make sure the Maidan was free of policemen— there was just a ragged old man leading a train of goats, and some urchins playing pickup cricket—I climbed up the ladder steps, found an inviting tree on the far side, gave Hassan a cheery wave, and slid down the trunk of a coconut palm on the inner side of the wall, into the heart of the barracks.

What then transpired is of little relevance. Suffice to say that all worked perfectly, especially when a young officer took to chatting with me, assuming I was there with permission, and took me for tea with the exalted figure of his commanding officer. And for the rest of the afternoon I was escorted around to see all the structures I had wanted to see, until finally the officer offered me his car, with the scarlet flags and crossed scimitars of his general's rank flying from the hood, to take me home.

"Grand Hotel?" he asked, assuming I had a room overlooking the Maidan, since that was what most visitors wanted. I nodded, since it was quite true that I was pinioned in that awful, morose monument of a lodging house. There was a bit of a fuss when I couldn't find the chit that I would have been issued had I come in through one of the gates, but it was assumed that I was just careless, and my escorting officer—and the fluttering of the red flag—eventually convinced the sentries to let me go, and they saluted smartly as I passed out through the tunnel. Within moments, I was blinking in the sunlight again as we drove across the outer edge of the park past the pool known as the Havildars' Tank and across the Polo Ground up to Strand Road and the river, and finally to where Hassan was waiting, quite patiently. The ladder, I noted, had been taken away.

What then followed was a moment of delightfully memorable drama. My escort, a young captain in the education corps, was chatting in Hindi with my driver; I was listening to them and nodding, making believe I understood. Then there was a sudden shout, and I saw to my amazement a truck, a large tanker, careering on two wheels across the roundabout on Napier Road (with its memorial to the man who invented logarithms), coming straight toward us. With superhuman speed we ran onto the grass and dove into a shallow ditch. The truck plowed without slowing into the two cars. There was an enormous explosion as hundreds of gallons of gasoline ignited in a spectacular fireball, overshooting the top of the wall where I had been walking only an hour before. Pieces of metal rained down onto the asphalt. Then there was silence, aside from the crackling of the flames.

The three of us got up and wiped off the dust. A man who identified himself as the truck driver ran up, smiling idiotically. "No one hurt!" he said. "Big *tamasha!*" *Much excitement.* He surveyed the wreck. The captain looked on morosely, wondering how he would explain the loss of his general's car. Hassan hissed that he thought, since a crowd was gathering, it might be prudent to get away. What about his own car? I asked. Insurance, he said, and grinned. *Not mine anyway. New one tomorrow.* And so we said farewell to the officer and walked casually off together, across the grass of the Maidan, across Casuarina Avenue and over the threadbare acres of the old Parade Ground.

The fury of the blazing wreck soon died away. The flames became invisible—a fire engine had come, and I could see jets of foam—and a waft of black smoke drifted and thinned across the river. The road traffic and the yelp of the riverboats faded to a hum.

I looked around once or twice. No one had followed us; no policemen to take statements or to wrap us up in the enfolding madness of the local bureaucracy. The meadowland quieted, until there was just the bleat of the goats and the sound of leather and ash as a clutch of cricket balls were hit around by the armies of urchin-boys. We watched some other lads play with kites. Then a man offered to tell my fortune, another asked to me sit and let him use a dangerous-looking bamboo instrument to remove unwanted objects from my ears, and finally, a young girl with a basket of marigolds stopped me and offered a garland for just a couple of rupees.

I bought one, bright droplets of moisture still glistening on its petals. The girl grinned with the whitest teeth as she placed the flowers around my neck. Her thin brown arms smelled nicely of dust and wood smoke and village life. And then Hassan and I walked over Chowringhee and ducked into the bar at the Grand where I had a beer to calm myself. He took a *nimbu-pani*, a sweet-lime juice and water, and we both said cheers and tried to still our sorely frazzled nerves.

You never know what'll happen on the Maidan, I said to Hassan, and he laughed until his eyes ran with tears, more with relief than at my joke.

For it wasn't a joke at all. The fourteen hundred acres that the British carved from their onetime capital of India have now been fully subsumed into the fabric of what is, depending on your point of view, either the most chaotically delightful city on the planet, or the ghastliest and most pestilential city in creation. And played out on those acres are examples of both the very best of India, and the very worst.

The Maidan is surrounded by great buildings, just as Central Park is (though for Maidan it is on three sides, not four; the Maidan's western side is that thick brown distributary of the lower Ganges). But whereas the New York park is surrounded by walls of generally unremarkable structures, the palisades around the Calcutta Maidan were by and large constructed for permanence and magnificence, being deliberately built in palatial style and with formidable looks, most made of marble and most originally colored white.

There is a wall of commerce on the eastern side, with the merchants and mansions of the street named Chowringhee. A second wall of great government buildings rises high on the Maidan's northern edge—huge palaces, courts, churches, barracks blocks. And to the south is the third side of the Maidan stockade, with the cathedral and the military hospital, the police academy and the mansion of Belvedere, where the Viceroy's deputy liked to live. There too, and most notably, like an immense half-deflated wedding cake, stands the vast marble monument to Queen Victoria, which quite dominates the Maidan, like a same-sized Taj Mahal a thousand miles away.

And there is something even more remarkable about the space than its extraordinary architecture. It is this: that though over the years militant Indians in their millions have used the Maidan as a gathering ground for protest and agitation—with many of their protests vehemently anti-British in tone and intention—not once have the relics and statues of the Victoria Memorial been harmed.

Elsewhere in the city, as in India more generally, most relics of the Raj are gone. Even Calcutta's name has been dropped, replaced by Kolkata. Yet in Victoria's memorial, bathed in floodlight through the night, there still stands Lord Curzon, tall and arrogant and British. There are the huge marble gates, most topped by British equestrians of heroic memory. In the museum is the lock of hair of this great viceregal wife and the surrendered sword of that vanquished vassal; there are the scrolls of victory and the portraits of soldier-conquerors from London and Glasgow and Bristol, as well as the immense statues of Victory and the smaller intimate renderings of the child-queen. All of them remain untouched, for all India to come and see, under the stern invigilation of guards who police the memorial as if it belonged to Gandhi-ji.

Between these three great white walls—or rather the off-white and peeling in places quite *gray* walls, since stucco needs expensive repairs, and marble picks up stains from polluting jute factories nearby—is the parkland itself. Here it stands, huge, empty of construction, still undeveloped, still open, and still resolutely unspoiled by corruption or by government fiat. And even though in truth it has been worn out and wearied by time and overuse, its grasses stubbed down to nothing by the passage of a billion *chappals*, it retains a sad magnificence. The Maidan has certain loveliness, a bounty, born of the simple fact that in a city that is such a nightmarish delirium of crowds, it is the one real, honest-to-god, open space. A place where one can lie down, gaze up, and see the sky.

There was a time when the British would use their Fort William field-of-fire gardens as keenly as the Danes might use Tivoli. Once it had tennis courts and riding paths, flower-filled meadows and, within the sight and smell of the river, golf links. There once was a tradition of the nightly British promenade with grandees—most of them jumped-up boxwallahs, it has to be said—dressed unsuitably in silk and taffeta, walking or riding along the grand boulevards between parade ground and polo field and cricket pitch, showing that despite the heat and sultry air, the stiff upper lip could be maintained, and the look of Empire kept ever imperturbable.

Now, all that are left are ghosts. The buildings remain, the river remains, the fort remains—and within and around, the acres have been mercifully shielded from the developers who have ravaged Calcutta, making so much of the city so unutterably disagreeable. The Maidan is there, still providing unending and blessed relief for the people of a difficult city (and for its animals: there are mongooses to be seen occasionally, jackals often, goats all the time). It is the one lung that allows the millions of Calcuttans to draw breath in a place that seems otherwise never to have the time for silence or reflection. You see people walking alone, expressions of a mysterious inner bliss on their faces. Without the Maidan, I sometimes think, Calcutta would go mad.

SOME WAY TO THE EAST OF THE PARK, at a traffic-crowded junction on the road that leads toward it from the grim huddles of tenements, lies a small and very ancient cemetery, Park Street Cemetery. Full of tombs ornate and grand, it is where perhaps the most mordant epitaph of Empire has been written—an epitaph that also offers, I like to think, some kind of small commentary on the Maidan itself, a place that once and still offers a degree of peace, so close along the road.

The lines are on a tomb of a young woman named Rose Aylmer. In a library in south Wales she had met a poet named Walter Savage Landor, and the pair had fallen in love. She had then come out to India, accompanying her parents, but died of dysentery in Calcutta soon after arriving, after eat-

213

ing too much unwashed fruit. She was twenty. Landor was distraught, and he remained heartbroken for the sixty-four years that he survived her.

He saw that she was properly buried, and then had eight precious lines inscribed on her gravestone. I always stop to look and to ponder these most beautiful of words. I now know them by heart. The cemetery, I feel, is a vital station for visitors to Calcutta. The words on Rose Aylmer's tomb should be read, I feel, by anyone who is thinking of walking west along Park Street, and who perhaps is then going on toward the river and the distant hush of the Maidan.

The two verses cut into the stone speak mainly to the savage brevity that so often marked out young life in India. But they also speak, I think, to the vital need for a kind of occasional peace, and which can only be attained in Calcutta in a very few places—one of them, most notably for these two lovers, in the great old fire-field park at the end of the cemetery road.

> *Ah what avails the sceptred race!*
> *Ah, what the form divine!*
> *What every virtue, every grace!*
> *Rose Aylmer, all were thine.*
>
> *Rose Aylmer, whom these wakeful eyes*
> *May weep, but never see,*
> *A night of memories and sighs*
> *I consecrate to thee*

The Maidan is surely such a place of memories and sighs. For all its curious origins, despite its weariness and raggedness and its worn-out grassland and crowds, and despite the mayhem all around it—truck crashes and fiery explosions included—it is precious, a place that deserves consecration, and for the sake of its city, to be preserved forever.

Maruyama Koen, Kyoto |
PICO IYER

A PUBLIC MONUMENT TO PRIVACY

I STEPPED OUT OF THE NEAR-SILENT BLACK TAXI and looked around. The low wooden gates of three-hundred-year-old temples stood on both sides of me, on a little lanterned lane barely wide enough to accommodate a car. A poem was inscribed on a four-foot-high gray rock, in flowing calligraphy, next to a stone pillar remembering a "guardian of the Emperor" who'd lived here. Five-story pagodas towered above the low walls at both ends of the narrow road, and around the corner was a cottage built by a haiku poet in honor of the great haiku master Bashō.

Night was falling, and I could barely make out a sound or shape in the deserted street. I might have been standing inside a Hiroshige woodcut. No one had told me, when I left my twenty-fifth-floor office in Rockefeller Center to come and live in Kyoto, that the ancient capital of Japan was more populous, more built up, often more noisy than Detroit. Yet in the vicinity of Maruyama Park I could forget all the commotion and step into something unfathomable.

From the windows of two-story teahouses I could hear soft laughter, occasionally see the ghost-white face of an apprentice geisha; pairs of twinned slippers at the entrance to a tiny restaurant spoke for chapter upon chapter of some unfolding romance. The café next to the little temple in which I was to take a room consisted of low tables next to which, cross-legged, I could watch giant, decades-old carp while sipping a green-tea float. The sanctuary across the street, created by the widow of the formidable sixteenth-century ruler Hideyoshi Toyotomi, helped mark the beginning of a pilgrim's quarter, leading up steep flights of steps to

Kiyomizu-dera, the Temple of Pure Water, commanding a hill overlooking all of Kyoto.

My second evening in the area, I slipped out of my small, bare tatami space and stole past the geishas' excited murmurs, along thin, white-globed lanes, to a phone booth plastered with pink stickers advertising company for the night. Around me were traditional teahouses, freshly washed pathways snaking between low hedges. Next to me, through a thirty-foot-high, orange torii gate, was a park, and as I walked into it I found myself inside a silent world of lights and huts barely lit by flaking sticks of incense.

At its southern entrance, Maruyama Park slips into a seventh-century shrine, Yasaka-jinja, whose central wooden platform is ringed by sixty bobbing white lanterns on every side. A woman—apparently from the adjoining geisha district of Gion, the "water world"—was standing alone in prayer in front of the main hall, hands joined, eyes tightly closed. I wandered past her to the center of the park and came upon a grove of eight hundred cherry trees around a single, majestic, weeping cherry that was, a sign told me, the most celebrated in Japan.

At its western entrance, ninety seconds away, another high, gray-tiled orange torii led out of the park into the very heart of Kyoto's clamorous downtown. To the north, the park leaked into a tiny street of vast, wooden temples: Chion-in next door is the place where the New Year is ritually tolled in, with 108 strokes each January 1, the central temple of the Jodo sect, representing the Pure Land school of Buddhism. And all around the edges of Maruyama Park were teahouses and traditional restaurants, many of them open only to those whose families had been associated with them for centuries; Kyoto's classic aesthetic cherishes an exquisiteness that's curtained and a community based upon everything that doesn't need to be said.

Metropolitan yet somehow mystical, full of familiar props in radically unfamiliar settings, Maruyama Park quickly came to embody for me precisely the sense of secludedness, the subtlety—the rich reticence—I'd come to Kyoto to try to absorb. It was like a public monument to privacy. But it was also a bridge, drawing together disparate influences from everywhere. I could almost hear, from the west, crowds gathering around the stores selling fans and lanterns and parasols and obi, along one of Kyoto's busiest shopping streets. But from the other side came the sonorous gongs of the Buddhist temples, as they have come for centuries. ("The bells of Gion Temple knell the impermanence of everything," as the famous first line of the classic *Tale of the Heike* intones.) And if I walked past Maruyama's swan pond, and zigzagged among its cherry trees, up a wide, irregular series of stone steps, past a thin waterfall, I'd find myself in one of the most hidden and mysterious entertainment quarters in the city, a spectral scatter of private restaurants and temples set around a bamboo forest.

I started going to Maruyama again and again, in the days that followed, as if to try to figure out the riddle that was my new home. After midnight, I came upon the few homeless people in the city, rolling out their mats in one sequestered corner of the park and sleeping in perfect rows, shoes tidily laid out at their feet, before making themselves scarce as soon as the light came up. In the daytime, couples were shopping for Hello Kitty socks near the pond, or dipping into brown-tea-and-tofu or green-tea-and-vanilla ice creams. Sometimes I saw men in glasses furiously shaking blond-wood cylinders out of which came a thin stick telling their future in life or in love.

There were no rolling lawns, as in the parks I'd grown up on in Oxford and New York City; there was no space for young ladies to ride horses or for boys to throw Frisbees. Haiku-brief, inward looking and mostly paved, Maruyama Koen (as it is called in Japanese) had no place for joggers or shortstops or sunbathers. It was more of a place for flâneurs and epicures, home to mostly grown-up pleasures: the site where the city's cultured night district dribbled off into spirit-filled hills, and no one could be sure what that young woman was whispering to that shaved-headed monk in the dark.

KYOTO, CAPITAL OF JAPAN from the year 794 to 1868, is a palimpsest city, a lesson in layers and veils; it tells you not to judge by appearances and not to presume you can read how deep an implication or connection might be.

When I first arrived in Maruyama Park, like many an unschooled newcomer, I took it to be a perfect emblem of the Meiji Period, at the turn of the twentieth century, when Japan suddenly began importing Western props that somehow made the country more Japanese than ever. The European restaurant that sits right next to a long pathway often flowing with girls in cotton kimono advertises a "Beer Garden" in the summer and now offers what it calls a "Tea Seminar." A wooden sign nearby tells you that Maruyama in its modern form was designed in 1913 by the landscape gardener Jihei Ogawa VII, who was also responsible for the gorgeous strolling garden in the Meiji-era Heian Shrine a few minutes to the north. At the center of the park's haphazard walkways stands a large statue of Ryoma Sakamoto and Shintaro Nakaoka, two of the celebrated samurai who lost their lives trying to bring the Meiji Reformation into being. And thus, as it happens, taking the court away from Kyoto and placing it in Tokyo, making Maruyama Park a reminder of departed glory—merely a "deserted place of shrubs and weeds," according to a sign—at the time when the city around it was a thriving capital.

But look closer. A tiny map at your feet points toward a hermitage, a "Dream Stone Monument" (apparently a great bell linked to the cherry blossoms) and the city's central graveyard, two minutes to the south. Look around you and you'll see statues of foxes, agents for the gods, and shrines tucked among the trees, above stone basins whose ladles invite you to clean your mouth and hands before you pray. Walk into the shrine and an elderly bald grandfather, in white and pale gray summer kimono, is teaching three toddlers, aged four or five, how to swing the worn rope and clap their hands twice to summon the gods.

A secular, international-seeming modern place filled with ancient memories and gods: how better to find a microcosm of Kyoto itself? The spiritual heart of Maruyama Park, after all, Yasaka Shrine—sometimes known as Gion Shrine—dates from 656, 138 years before there was even a city here. In this very spot, it's said, the hot-tempered Shinto god of sea and storms, Susano, chanced to visit the humble home of an ordinary man, and was so moved by the hospitality afforded him that he promised protection from pestilence and prosperity to the man and his family forever.

As a result, Yasaka Shrine became the place where everyone came to pray for divine assistance as Kyoto began to take shape. By the turn of the first millennium, it was a shrine to which the emperor sent messengers when he wanted to pass on news from court to the Shinto gods. Nowadays, each December 28, a sacred fire is struck at the hour of the tiger—4 A.M.—and from it votive lanterns are lit; visitors during the New Year's celebration take parts of the auspicious flame, on strands of rope, back to their little altars at home. In spring, people crowd in to inspect the often bare, almost witchy tree at the park's center suddenly lit up, thick with pink, frothing blossoms, and hundreds of businessmen, in loosened ties, sit under the flowers and belt out bawdy songs over cans of beer. In autumn, as you look up from beside its pond at Mount Maruyama to the east, you can see the full blaze of reds and golds, against deep blue skies, as if to shed light on the Buddhist idea of constant change against a canvas of changelessness.

Even when nothing is going on, the place seems alive as only a miniature swarming with details can be. As the cicadas buzz deafeningly one morning in midsummer, I come upon four older men—relics of last night's revelry, or just early risers discussing the day's prospects, it's hard to tell. A woman in Dior is hurrying home through the park, looking away from a stranger's eyes, yet fully in possession of herself.

I associate parks in most cities with sunshine and the suddenly loosened excitement of stripping off extra layers and going out to enjoy daylight and space. But Maruyama is a more formal place, made for dressing up, not down. It's best savored at dusk, when lights come on around the teahouses in its corners, and darkness deepens above the benches. Japanese sentences tend to trail off for maximum implication, and so it is with the walkways that dawdle for maybe three minutes across the park and then disappear among the hushed streets that lead to a small graveyard, Anyoji Temple, and a shrine honoring a goddess associated with music.

I LIKE TO GO TO MARUYAMA, therefore, on misty days, a quarter century after I first came upon the park. It's a place for reading Junichiro Tanizaki's essay in praise of shadows, or seeing the clouds veil then reveal the hills a few minutes away, remaking the space every moment. When I need to spend a night in the city, visiting from my new home ninety minutes away, I stay in a traditional inn just outside the park's southern entrance, and sample the incense museum that now exists next door, the shop that sells nothing but owls. When visitors come from overseas, I make sure to take them through Maruyama Park, not because there's anything special to see there, but because not looking for something to see, simply inhaling the atmosphere and finding pleasure in the everyday, is the way to get the most out of recessive Japan.

The ideal approach to the place, I think, is to set aside all words and head up its great steps on a late afternoon at the end of November. Walk past the growling lions on both sides of the western torii, past the bright red festival stands selling fried octopus balls, past the vestal virgins, all in white, selling charms for success in exams and protection against traffic accidents, and then past the European pond with swans barely visible in the dusk.

The whole of Maruyama is alight in the last fiery glow of late afternoon, golden light slicing through the trees, and at the back of the park you'll come to a manicured mini-forest that seems to have been forgotten by the world. Kimonoed silhouettes are just beginning to stir behind the paper screens of a nearby restaurant. The chill of winter is coming into the air. You can almost feel the approaching dark. Sit down, catch your breath, and listen to the great bell of Chion-in summoning robed men to prayer. It's only when you can't see much at all that Maruyama—like the city around it—comes most deeply into its own.

Park Güell, Barcelona |
COLM TÓIBÍN

THERE ARE NO STRAIGHT LINES in nature, Antoni Gaudí said. Thus, when he designed the Park Güell in Barcelona, he saw no reason why there should be straight lines in architecture.

I came to Barcelona first in September 1975, when the idea of city tourism—unless it was a honeymoon in Paris, or a pilgrimage to Rome—was unheard-of in Europe. You went to the beaches on your holidays then and lay in the sun. Thus the city of Barcelona was undiscovered territory. There were no guidebooks, and the natives of the city took its beauty for granted.

Park Güell is on a hill overlooking the city, surrounded by middle-class apartments. In the years when I first knew the city no one made a fuss about Gaudí. Progressive people in Barcelona disliked the unfinished church of La Sagrada Família, which he had worked on exclusively over the last decade or more of his life; people believed it was a waste of money and overwrought in its tone and texture.

It was a time when people wanted to be cool; they wanted rational politics and rationalist architecture. And the idea of an architect comfortable working for rich clients or the Catholic Church, as Gaudí did, did not fit with politics in Barcelona after the death of the dictator Francisco Franco in November 1975.

The park was waiting to be discovered. When I first found it, I was strolling in the conventional streets that run off Plaça Lesseps and innocently ventured in. It was a chilly day in spring with a lovely pure, thin light that comes in Barcelona on days when the sky is blue but the summer has not yet come. I was attracted at first by the tiling on the walls outside, and then by the bizarre shape of the two gate lodges. But it was when I came to the forest of stone where the tree shapes incline, as though in a mad fairy-tale drawing or a strange dream, that I realized I was in space created by a brilliant mind, someone who managed to create new and skewed rules that, as you moved up through the paths of the park, become more and more intriguing.

Yet much of the layout of Park Güell, which Gaudí designed and put in place between 1900 and 1914, is superbly organized. The terraces, the pathways, as well as the vegetation and the views of the Mediterranean and the city below, come from serious thought and planning, as does the system of irrigation. All the detail, on the other hand—the use of stone and concrete and tiling—is exotic and fearless, at times crazy and overwhelming, and also puzzling and unsettling.

Gaudí was as interested in nature as he was in culture, and more fascinated by God than he was by man. The main esplanade, which stretches out over the park, is surrounded by benches that roll and curl like waves of the sea. Some of the images in the park are openly religious, almost devotional.

The benches are remarkably comfortable—since Gaudí went to considerable lengths to make them restful, creating their form close to the shape of the body when seated—and made of broken ceramic tiles. The mosaic looks as though some shards and fragments were found and someone was foolish enough to put them all together again—restored rather than created. The effect is ingenious and fascinating. Sometimes there is a pattern; sometimes there is none. Some colors predominate—shades of blue and some gold. Some of the shapes take their bearing from nature; others are more abstract or geometric. Nearby is the walkway that I have come to love: a strange petrified forest with trees made of stone that seem to grow, creating a shadowy and unsettling space to move in. Nothing can be depended upon.

In many ways, Park Güell represents the tensions within Gaudí's own complex soul. Often, as he worked, he forgot his religious conviction when he saw a chance to be anarchic. For example, underneath the large terrace where the whirling benches done in broken ceramic were built, he created a dramatic space with eighty-six columns—a somber atmosphere that evokes a temple. On its roof he placed circles of colored tiles, designed by Josep Maria Jujol, in intervals. To me, these are the most mysterious and beautiful creations in the entire park, with exquisite colors and suggestive shapes. Some of them are abstract, ambiguous; others echo the shape of the moon and the stars. In all of them the color and the design are richly mysterious, clearly done by a great ceramic artist. For example, the wonderful salamander in ceramic tiles is a centerpiece of great color and imaginative energy.

THE LAYOUT OF THE PARK, the use of material, the particular shapes and fantastic structures, arose from a need to forge a distinct Catalan identity at the end of the nineteenth and the beginning of the twentieth century. The Catalans prided themselves on using the most modern building systems while also evoking a sense of lost medieval grandeur. The spirit of Catalonia itself, the nation, was evoked in an architectural movement known as Modernism, in which Gaudí was a central figure. In this movement, wild dreams were given substance; rich conservative clients wanted what was original and strange. This was part of a yearning to create a nation, as Catalonia became increasingly wealthy and the city of Barcelona itself became much larger.

At the turn of the century young architects and their clients began to compete with each other to create the most exciting and outlandish buildings. Wagnerian iconography, Art Nouveau floral patterns, and sumptuous decoration all became part of the new city's style.

Gaudí believed that the best way to get to know a man was by spending his money, and he judged that the Catalan industrialist Eusebi Güell, for whom Gaudí worked almost thirty years beginning in 1885, was "a gentleman in every sense of the word." In 1885 Gaudí built Güell a palace off the Ramblas in the old city. Gaudí also became chief architect of the Sagrada Família, the church that would remain unfinished at the time of his death in 1926. Gaudí was also changing from being a fashionable figure, a man who lived well and dressed well, to becoming a solitary, difficult, and deeply religious man, ascetic and puritan in his personal habits. By the mid-1890s he began to go on long fasts. As his clothes and his living quarters became more drab, Gaudí's imagination flourished. Living at one extreme of poverty in a city that valued wealth allowed his interior life an extraordinary richness.

Gaudí, who was lucky to have enough work to sustain him all his life in Barcelona, left Catalonia very little. But Eusebi Güell traveled extensively, and carried back news about design and architecture in Germany and England. It was through Güell, for example, that Gaudí became acquainted with the work of William Morris and his English contemporaries. It was through Güell that Gaudí also became aware of the idea of a garden city.

Güell wanted to promote the idea of a Catalonia closer in spirit to England and Germany than to Castile or Andalusia; of a place separate from Spain in its industriousness and in its attitude toward modernity and innovation, culture and design. Thus Gaudí's work on the park suited Güell's political and economic vision. While Gaudí's vision can seem wild and theatrical, it also was conservative. His park, as much as his buildings, was filled with meanings and narratives essentially Catholic and invoking the Catalan past.

Güell died in 1918 and the park was bought by the city in 1922, four years before Gaudí's death. From the terraces of the park, you can see the towers of the Sagrada Família rising, and other houses in the city below—including La Pedrera on Passeig de Gràcia—that Gaudí designed.

Being in Park Güell requires careful attention. It has different moods, some of them filled with openness and brightness, others more somber, almost eerie. It is still for me at its most beautiful in early spring, when the light against the tiles is more slanted and tourism is less intense. Gaudí's initial dream was for the park to be private, used only by those who bought sites and built houses in its grounds, and it is lovely when you can find it almost empty. It is a tribute to the work of a great image maker, who believed it was part of his patriotic duty to make dream spaces where the mind could contemplate beauty and eternity and mystery as well as the chaos and disorder of the world. It has a way of making me slow down, look at things more carefully, relish color and shape, and relish the city of Barcelona itself, of which this park is an essential and exquisite element.

Parque Ecológico de Xochimilco,
Mexico City |

DAVID LIDA

A CANAL IS NOT A CANAL
IS NOT A CANAL

THE MAN SEATED NEXT TO ME on the plane had a Jesus look. In his early twenties, he was pale with longish hair, a beard, and a troubled expression. It turned out he was a native of Mexico City, where we were both headed. Still in my twenties myself in those days, I had passed through the city once before and had fallen in love with what I saw (although I'd only stayed overnight). Now I would be there for a month. I asked Jesus a question that I find dreadfully annoying when it's put to me: what he recommended I do and see when I got to his hometown.

He didn't seem to mind being asked, although his answers were mostly obvious. Of course I couldn't miss the Anthropology Museum. I should go to Coyoacán on a Sunday afternoon. The Rivera murals, the Pyramid of the Sun, the Palace of Fine Arts. A couple of other suggestions came as surprises. He insisted I must eat *tacos al pastor*—seasoned pork roasted on a revolving spit like *shwarma*, then served in a tortilla with onion, cilantro, and pineapple. And I shouldn't leave Mexico City without going to Xochimilco.

The young man—incredibly, his name was in fact Jesús—wrote down the word for me. Xochimilco. As with many foreigners, my first adventure was with its pronunciation. In fact, it sounds almost exactly the way it looks. So-chee-*meel*-co. I asked Jesús what it meant, what I would be going to see. Words failed him. It is a shortcoming of the human race that when we describe one place, we invariably measure it up against another. That may be all you need if you're comparing the red-light districts of different Mexican border towns, the sand on any beach in the Dominican Republic, or every burg of fewer than twenty thousand people in east Texas. Jesús compared Xochimilco to Venice. I've since learned that people *always* compare Xochimilco to Venice, when in fact the two places have nothing in common but canals.

XOCHIMILCO IS ONE OF SIXTEEN delegations (the equivalent of arrondissements in Paris, or boroughs in London or New York) that make up the Federal District, the enormous, palpitating heart of Mexico City. Xochimilco used to be a separate town, but it was one of the many localities enveloped by the urban sprawl that turned Mexico City into a monster of about 22 million souls in the last fifty years. In Xochimilco alone, there are close to half a million residents and about fifty neighborhoods.

But when people talk about Xochimilco, they're usually referring to a network of canals—extending more than a hundred miles—that snake through certain parts of the district. This is where Jesús sent me, to one of nine docks where tourists—mostly locals on a day off—board wooden boats called *trajineras*, painted yellow and red and covered in battered tin ceilings. A *trajinera* is something in between a canoe and a gondola, and is driven by a cinnamon-skinned boatman who plunges a wooden pole into the shallow water, pushing off against the muddy bottom.

On either side of the water are what are known in indigenous Náhuatl as *chinampas*—man-made islands affixed to the bottom of the lakebed. People live on these islands among the grass and trees, some in solid constructions of brick and concrete, others in makeshift shanty shacks of clapboard and corrugated tin. Mostly they grow flowers—the *chinampas* are full of greenhouses, through which you can occasionally glimpse explosions of red roses, purple bougainvillea, yellow acacias, blue forget-me-nots. Indeed, in Náhuatl, the word Xochimilco means "the fertile terrain where flowers grow."

I went to the canals on a Sunday, which was a shock. Sunday is when most Mexican families are likely to be off from work and school, and it seemed like all 22 million citizens were in Xochimilco at once. So many *trajineras* crept along that the canals were as clogged as the Periférico or the Circuito Interior—the perpetually jammed inner-city throughways that ring Mexico City.

Still, being stuck in a *trajinera* was a lot more amusing than a taxi during rush hour. The roofs of the boats were festooned with colorful arches, adorned with women's names—Lupita, Laurita, Linda Renata; María de los Ángeles, María del Rosario, María del Pilar. Extended families with dozens of members filled the boats, from the grandparents slowly sipping tequila at tables in the center, to infants perilously hanging from the edges, dipping their hands in the brackish water. A teenage boy in one boat narrowed his eyes in his best approximation of a smoldering stare, while a girl in an adjoining vessel resolutely ignored him.

Her boat was doing its best to pass his in what was more or less the right lane of maritime traffic. The maneuver was complicated by a tiny *trajinera* bearing a mariachi band in black studded suits that had attached itself to the boy's family's boat and was entertaining the group with a serenade of the song "La Bikina," with blasting trumpets and stirring violins. They drowned out the competing noise of a marimba band in another boat, its trilling xylophone demure in comparison.

A woman in a passing rowboat dipped an oar in the water while her husband yodeled a sales pitch for ears of corn, roasted or boiled in a huge pot, slathered with mayonnaise and powdered chili. Other vendors sold miniature models of *trajineras*, bouquets of flowers, or the opportunity of being photographed while wearing a tasseled sombrero with a humongous brim. The traffic problem was exacerbated by *trajineras*, which would abruptly pull over to a *chinampa* and wait while people left the boats to use primitive toilet facilities for a couple of pesos.

DURING THAT EXCURSION, no Mexican family offered me the chance to thrust myself into its bosom. Nor would I have, out of shyness, had the opportunity arose. Nonetheless, I felt I had missed out on something: I had experienced alone, as an outsider, what would ideally have been a shared experience. A year or so later, I had moved to Mexico City, and soon had a chance to return to Xochimilco with the first friends I made: two brothers from a village in Austria who had come to live in the city a few years earlier, their respective girlfriends, their best friend, who was Mexican, and his wife, as well as a Mexico City native whom I'd later marry.

They knew the lay of the land. As soon as we boarded the *trajinera*, the Austrians commanded the boatman to take us on an insider's tour. As quickly as possible he steered us away from the canals bustling with tourists and took us toward the back roads, so to speak.

In minutes, we were alone along the waterways. Gone were the screaming families, the itinerant musicians, the vendors of knickknacks, gewgaws, and bagatelles. Now, a mere eleven miles from the central square of downtown Mexico City, we were in the country—a scene so pastoral that I couldn't imagine I was anywhere near a megalopolis, let alone within one. Across the passing *chinampas* we saw fields of cactus, corn, chili peppers, and wildflowers. On the banks of black, fertile earth, children fished for minnows with plastic buckets, while skinny dogs, tethered to trees so they wouldn't drown, barked plaintive greetings. Wild ducks paddled alongside for what seemed like miles, hoping for a handout from the picnic we'd packed.

White herons glided around us, occasionally dropping into the water, to emerge with flat, oily perch in their narrow yellow beaks. A snake slithered up from a thick patch of water lilies. We passed a workshop where workmen built and repaired *trajineras*, and once in a while a rowboat would pass, bearing a man with a wheelbarrow full of dirt or a cluster of potted plants. Occasionally, police in motorized boats drove by, nodding at us with smiles on their faces, on what I imagined was the most peaceful detail in Mexico City. It was a remarkably clear day, and by the time we reached the Cuemanco Canal a couple of hours later, we had a spectacular view of Popocatépetl and Iztaccíhuatl, the two monumental volcanoes south of Mexico City, under a cloudless, crystalline sky.

The Austrians had packed a picnic for the four hours we rode back and forth—roast chickens they'd bought at a bakery, along with fresh cactus and carrot salads. Shots of tequila were poured liberally from a bottle they'd brought, and we also drank beer that had been procured for us by the boatman at the dock. Along the ride, we parked at a *chinampa* and the boatman dispatched a local to find us a bucket of pulque—a viscous drink favored by the Aztecs, made from fermented but undistilled cactus and flavored with fresh guava. If the drinks were Mexican, the music that the Austrians blared from their boom box (mostly Pavarotti singing "O Sole Mio," plus selections from the other Two Tenors) was decidedly not.

Before turning back, we would stop at a creepy *chinampa* known as the Island of the Dolls. The story went that some forty years earlier, a man named Señor Julián heard the cries of a woman drowning in the canal. He dove in the water and swam toward her, but she died before he could save her. Afterward, he would hear her crying perpetually during the night. As a talisman to ward off her spirit, he began to hang dolls from the trees by the water.

Throughout the decades, Julián became a Xochimilco legend, and people brought him dolls from far and wide. Today there are hundreds of them, suspended from trees, metal wires, and the walls of the dilapidated shacks on his property. They look like images that might have appeared in a nightmare or a low-budget horror film. Some are green with verdigris; many are naked. Others, with matted, windswept hair, crawl with vermin. Señor Julián died in 2005, and now his nephew administers the place, selling shots of tequila and telling his uncle's tale to whoever will listen.

I CONFESS THAT, TO THIS DAY, I have never been to Venice, for fear of being crushed amid a throng of tourists. But I have seen so many films and read so much literature set there that I feel as if I know it all too well. Venice is Katharine Hepburn falling backward into the canal in *Summertime* or Julie Christie and Donald Sutherland pursued by a knife-wielding homunculus in *Don't Look Now*. It's where Shylock beseeched Portia for a pound of Antonio's flesh, where a sinister gondolier assured Von Aschenbach that "il signore will pay" for his ride, and where, in *The Wings of the Dove*, out of respect for the doomed Milly Theale, Morton Densher offered Kate Croy a hauntingly disappointing bargain. I fear that to go there would be to visit a grand decaying center of Europe, a museum whose inhabitants have their palms perpetually extended to collect from tourist purses.

None of those images recall Xochimilco—at least not to my mind. Above all, a ride through Xochimilco is a quick and inexpensive trip to the sixteenth century, a glimpse of what the Spaniards saw when they conquered Mexico City—a largely placid, locally sustainable civilization built on a lakebed, where flora and fauna were either caught in the wild or raised, grown, and consumed, and where commerce was conducted by boat between *chinampa* and *chinampa*. It is a testament to the undying vibrancy of primordial Mexican culture.

The Presidio, San Francisco |
ANDREW SEAN GREER

WHAT IF YOU FELL IN LOVE? Let's say 1990 in San Francisco, the earthquake rubble cleared up now, the fallen freeways restored or tagged for removal. Perhaps you drive your grandmother's red Buick Skyhawk—the one whose engine is one month short of throwing a rod outside of Winnemucca, Nevada—on Arguello Street through the grand concrete entrance to the Presidio. The road spins in a semicircle past the golf course, dips down, and then the city is gone. All around is a vast, dark eucalyptus and Monterey pine forest and a sense of a forbidden zone, a military base abandoned only a year before, and even as you pass the stunning vista of the Golden Gate lit by the sun, you find yourself passing rows of empty officers' quarters, and picnic tables, and know that somewhere to the east is that barren square where so recently soldiers bowled, and ate, and bought PX supplies. Roll down the windows and you can smell the trees, the damp, cool, camphorated shadows of the ghost garrison. Who knows who runs it now? There is not a soul anywhere. Down, beneath the giant trees, where Immigrant Point provides your first glimpse of the Pacific, rolled out flat as tin with a motionless Chinese cargo ship, then another loop until you are on Lincoln Boulevard and nothing blocks the view now. Ocean, and the Golden Gate, and across it: the sleeping form of Marin's golden mountains, tipped by the lighthouse at Point Bonita. Stop there; use the untrustworthy handbrake. Turn and look at him smiling at you, the water gleaming behind him. You are twenty years old. It is summer and somehow hot as you always imagined California to be. Sometimes, you get the day you want.

THE PRESIDIO WAS NOT ALWAYS A FOREST. Dial back two hundred years, and you would be standing on dunes and scrub grass. Here, on Cantil Blanco, Captain Juan Bautista de Anza stood with an advance guard and a Franciscan priest and planted a cross at the northernmost outpost of the empire of King Charles II of Spain, proclaiming that a new presidio would be built. *Presidio*, from the Roman encampments: *praesidium*. Here, with a view of the sea and invading ships. "I think," the priest wrote in his diary, "that if it could be well settled like Europe there would not be anything more beautiful in all the world. . . ."

Through distant wars, the fortifications changed hands to Mexico, then at last to the United States, which meant little more to the men there than the changing of flags on the flagpole. In that time, it had become a cold and windy punishment for misbehaving soldiers, a hardship outpost, visited only once a year by a supply ship. It was so ill-provided that when a Russian frigate fired a friendly shot, the San Franciscans had to row out to the ship to borrow powder in order to fire one in return. The presidio, in fact, had not even been built on the place De Anza chose. After he returned to Mexico, his lieutenant decided the spot was too windy, so he built it a mile southeast. That building was abandoned by 1835, and the cold wet fog began to wear down the old adobe walls. Later, those walls were hauled off to build a customs house. And thus little was left of that old Spanish presidio, in the wide sand dunes, now denuded of scrub grass and trees by cattle and logging to supply the city now booming to the south.

SAY YOU GOT OUT OF THE CAR into the hot, buzzing air with the distant hush of the surf below. He gets out, too, and stretches, facing away from you toward the water, then stands, hands in pockets. Always: hands in pockets.

A plain blue T-shirt, and plain tan shorts. Broad and manly, with a strong-jawed English face whose slightly parted lips reveal a Rhode Island accent. Short black hair and, in fact, short. Taller in memory, but five foot five today. Silhouetted against a view unimaginable months ago. The first time your brother took you out to see the cliffs, you thought: "This has been going on all this time? And no one told me?" The sky blue, all blue, and just the haze of a marine layer out at sea that later would come in to mantle the city. The picnic's in the backseat. Perhaps a bag of deli sandwiches, salami, hard cheese, bread, and nectarines. Who can remember? Surely a splurge of some kind: pâté. Grab the bag and he says I'll carry it and you say I've got it. Slam the door and walk around to join him, pretending you can see the view when all you see is the view inside yourself, of him so close, not holding your hand. And then he holds your hand. "Let's go," he says, and you walk to where a dirt path begins, downward. You will not know for hours that the keys are locked in the car.

States have a state rock and California's is serpentine. It is what this is all made of, covered by sand and dirt, but as you descend the path with its mere rope rail, it's the serpentine that shows itself in the cliffside: blue-green. And beyond it, appearing from the east: the Golden Gate Bridge. A scarf of vapor caught in one bright tower. He is no longer holding your hand; it is 1990, and he was raised in Rhode Island, where such things are hard to get used to, even in San Francisco. He climbs down ahead of you, and you watch his dark head bobbing with each step down the sand-stairs to Battery Crosby. His name is Neil. He is twenty-six years old—a man.

I CAN'T REMEMBER WHOSE IDEA IT WAS to spend that summer in San Francisco. My friend Eve's? Surely not my twin brother's. Surely not mine alone. But junior year of college was closing down, and like any decision the young make, it was done quickly, sloppily, happily: they would drive the Skyhawk

265

across the country and I would fly out to meet them. Eve's cousin had ex-tra rooms to rent—at two hundred dollars a month—in some place called the Mission. And this was to be my "wild" summer. I had been through two tough boyfriends—one who wouldn't love me, one who wouldn't sleep with me—and I felt that was enough. Though it was the era of AIDS and sex terrified me (we did not know what, if anything, was safe), still I had wild oats to sow. And then, in the last week before my departure, I met Neil. In a shopping mall, in a furniture store (what furniture could I need?), he stared at me from the across the room, then called me up that night. He lived in my college town and had seen me around; he knew exactly who I was. We went for coffee. He called and called. I had never in my young life been so pursued by someone so handsome. "Should I date him?" I asked my room-mate. She stared at me. "He's a Greek god," she pronounced. He was—darkly gorgeous, masculine, confident.

One night, Neil drove me to a beach near his hometown and produced a bottle of champagne. I sowed a few wild oats that night. But I was still re-sistant. Neil said many nice things that night, and asked me why I wouldn't be with him. I couldn't say. "What would you change about me?" he asked, almost pleading. I recall thinking about it for a moment, looking at him na-ked in the moonlight on that beach. "I would make your eyes blue," I said. How is it possible I would be so cruel?

But his pursuit won out. I was still so young, beaten by many rejec-tions (when I asked my last boyfriend why he wouldn't sleep with me, he said, "I couldn't decide if you were attractive enough") and to be adored, cherished, beloved—I desired that so much more than sex. By the time my brother picked me up in San Francisco, and drove me through that foreign landscape into the Mission, I had promised Neil to be his only. Three thou-sand miles away. It was not to be a wild summer, after all. We entered Army Street, a parade of brightly colored houses, and turned onto Dolores and its

Victorians, its people lazing in the park, its impossible palm trees against the blue sky. San Francisco. It was to be my summer of love.

IT WAS ONLY IN THE 1880S, after the success of turning a sandy stretch of land into Golden Gate Park, that the military began to take interest in changing the dunes in the Presidio. Major W. A. Jones wrote a proposal for an enormous tree planting program to transform the army's land: "In order to make the contrast from the city seem as great as possible," he wrote, "and indirectly accentuate the idea of the power of the Government, I have surrounded all the entrances with dense masses of wood." His only warning, in this careful design, was against planting crowds of trees at random. Three years later, he was transferred away. And the military began to plant crowds of trees at random.

The change was an affront to neighbors, and a shock to one impressionable young lad who grew up on its borders. He was "devastated," he wrote, when the Army Corps of Engineers tore down the native live oaks he loved; he was only eight years old. Later, he would fight against all plans for forestation in the landscape he loved: "I cannot think of a more tasteless undertaking than to plant trees in a naturally treeless area, and to impose an interpretation of natural beauty on a great landscape that is charged with beauty and wonder, and the excellence of eternity." His name was Ansel Adams.

Major Jones himself returned in the next century, alarmed at what he had wrought so many years before. Closely packed groves, forests that squeezed out sunlight and variety, the "dense masses of wood" he had proscribed. His only advice to the military was to leave the dunes that remained "just as they are."

And so from nothing the forest was built when I arrived, that warm day in 1990, and experienced the cool peppermint-scented mystery of the place, with him beside me as it opened into a vista blocked for a century. Impossible to imagine, before. And now: impossible to imagine it being any other way.

WALK OVER ABANDONED BATTERY CROSBY, the gun long since removed, and down the steep staircase to where a flat rock gives you a picnic view of the water. Not here, though, but down to the right along a path through tall bushes that passes over broken serpentine fragments and a wooden bridge. A sign to the beach and Neil stops you there: who wouldn't kiss him? It has been a long pursuit, and he has won. Nobody here to see. Hand in hand now, you make your way across boulders and pounding waves to an isolated stretch of sand and stone. Above it: the bridge. Beside it: the surf and sea and sun.

You spread out the towels, one white, and one blue, from the cousin's apartment over Modern Times Bookstore. You spent all the temp money you made this month on a meal last night at the best restaurant you could think of, Zuni Café, a glass triangle at the juncture of Market and Valencia, and who could forget prying each periwinkle from its lavender shell with a toothpick, dipping it in aioli, feeding it to each other? Side by side at a narrow table; you had never sat that way in a restaurant before. It felt elegant and grown-up. And here: side by side on towels, naked in the sun. Surf washing in, iced tea cold in a thermos. And someone loves you. The night that Neil arrived, he told you he didn't like protection during sex, it wasn't intimate, and you could trust each other. There was no cure or treatment in that time for the danger you might face; there was only death. But in the darkness, what lover would be bold enough to say, "I won't"?

THE PRESIDIO ALSO HOLDS thorns of war for this city of peace. It was here, in first growth of this eucalyptus forest, that all four Buffalo soldier regiments assigned to the Pacific during the Spanish-American War departed and returned. Two of those African-American regiments were garrisoned here, and in this full-grown forest some remain: four hundred of them, buried in the Presidio's cemetery. Here General Dewitt oversaw the internment of thousands of Japanese Americans, while on the beach, at the airport of Crissy Field (built first as a racetrack), Japanese-American soldiers worked on translating and decoding enemy messages. After the war, the Golden Gate's Nike missile defense system was headquartered in the Presidio, commanding the silos buried across the water in those golden hills. Herb Caen, the *San Francisco Chronicle* narrator of midcentury San Francisco, described the Presidio in the 1960s as full of mystery; the only sign of life was a general being driven from its gates, "taking salutes, nodding slightly, lordly as a conqueror in a chariot." That is what I picture, when I think of them closing the military base: that general taking his salutes. The National Park Service took over in 1994, but in 1990 it was still nobody's land. Not a base, not a park. A ghost town that San Franciscans wandered into warily, furtively, to sneak down to the beach below the Golden Gate Bridge.

AFTERWARD, YOU WILL TRUDGE BACK UP the bluff and find the car keys locked inside. This is the second time you've done this on this trip, and Neil stands on the grass, arms crossed, as you wait for AAA to come—again—and open the car with their little device. A fog will roll in between you. Something will change. Is it just the car, your distraction, your irresponsibility? Your clinging hand in his, your irritating chatter and pompous proclamations on the world? Is no one forgiven for being young? Or is it merely that moment on the beach, when Neil looked at you and smiled with secret pleasure, knowing he had won you utterly? It could be, for some, that passion has been purchased there and then one wisely walks away.

Still a clinging goodbye at the airport. Still a phone call every night, then every few nights, then a fellow hard to get in touch with three thousand miles away. No cell phones in 1990. No email. Another desperate message left on an answering machine. But everyone knows you cannot get out of

269

quicksand by struggling against it. You and Neil had talked of going to his brother's wedding in September. You had talked of moving together to an apartment above a grocery store. There is no explanation ever given. The panic of something lost, but perhaps still lying somewhere in grass, still salvageable, and so you are on your knees until the dusk.

Only later will you hear of other lovers Neil had that summer. Among them, one whose heart he broke as cleanly as he broke yours. Of all unlikely things: your last boyfriend, the one who would not sleep with you. Somehow you will laugh at that one.

In September, the Skyhawk pawned in Winnemucca, the summer money all spent, a long train ride up the Atlantic Coast to your last school year, you will be standing on Neil's porch a few blocks from the dormitories, staring at the sidewalk. Unwatered plants in pots around you. The very solid presence of him a foot away: those parted lips, those small brown eyes. The woody scent of his cologne. "What are you going to tell your friends?" he says at last in his deep voice. You cannot look at him. Your heart and life in mortal danger now, working just to stay alive. "I'm going to tell them you went insane." He nods.

IN 1806, IT IS SAID that Count Rezanov of Russia, in search of trade in sea otter coats, visited the Spanish Presidio and fell in love with the commandante's daughter, Concepción Arguëllo. They became engaged, and he headed back to Russia to close up his affairs there, promising to return and begin a life with her. They bid goodbye outside the Presidio fortress. But he did not return.

AND FIFTEEN YEARS LATER, a phone call. Living in San Francisco, near my brother and friend Eve, for whom that summer also had too magical a pull. Sitting on my corduroy sofa in the Mission: "Hi, Andy, it's Neil." How to explain the feeling, the rush of chemicals kept bottled on the shelf for so long, now tumbling down and breaking inside me? Nothing to do but laugh; I survived. "You know," I will say, nothing to win or lose now, "of all the voices I ever thought would make my heart race if I heard them again, yours is top of the list." A deep laugh I had also forgotten. What is he, forty or so now? Why on earth is he calling? Is it regret, after all this time? Or a whistle, calling back something that once was his? What thin blond boy is he remembering and trying to conjure up again? I am thirty-five. That boy doesn't live here anymore. "I'm sorry, Neil," I will tell him. "I have to go. I have to pick up my husband from the airport."

Of course, that is the last I will ever hear from him.

BUT THERE IS STILL this single day:

The wind blowing warm through the Monterey pines onto your bodies. A quick dip in the water proves it colder than anyone on the east coast could imagine, but there's something to shivering and laughing and drying oneself on a towel in the sun. Joking and running along the beach beside a boulder. He reapplies your sunscreen; he wears none himself. He kisses you, then lies back down. Facing you as he lies on the towel, so dark and tan; you would not wish his eyes blue now. There is still this. Where before was scrub and sand dune, now is this dense dark thicket. A wedding, a place together. Impossible to imagine, before. And now, looking across to where he smiles and takes your hand: impossible to imagine it being any other way. What else in life feels this way? What does it matter how things go? Be there for a moment more, Andy; be that boy in love.

"Quiet ecstasy and sweet content, why are not all days like you?" the poet James Schuyler wrote. "Happy with someone, and that someone you, together on a blue towel on sand beside the sea."

There is still this perfect day in the Presidio.

Prospect Park, Brooklyn |
NICOLE KRAUSS

[1]

FIRST THE DOGS: suddenly unleashed, quickened by the prospect of new discoveries, full to bursting with the moment at hand. Beginning at dawn, they pour into the park from all directions to rule over the sensational green sweep of Long Meadow. Dogs! Those "objects of insatiable interest," as Bruno Schulz called them, "examples of the riddle of life, created, as it were, to reveal the human being to man himself." They surge through the grass and under the trees in pursuit of balls, squirrels, or a smell that stirs something in the hidden regions of memory. They pause only to frisk each other for unpublished ideas, then return to the business of fresh experience. After an eternity of contemplation on the parquet floor, there is nothing that doesn't pique their interest.

Far off, at the edges of this happy panorama, a keen observer might catch sight of a sour or disgruntled face; not everyone shares an interest in the revelations of dogs. But such people have no recourse here and the dogs' rights are secure. After all, it's they who first ventured back into Prospect Park when everyone else was afraid to and, tails wagging, awash in slobber, conquered it back acre by acre from the dark forces. So let no one curse a dog here. Even one whose poop, uncollected, comes to decorate the bottom of a shoe. Even one who pees on an infant's stroller. On the infant himself.

At 9 a.m. sharp, the leashes are snapped on, and these furry examples of the riddle of life suddenly become something less doglike and—with an air of tired resignation—more human.

[2]

MY FATHER WAS RAISED IN BROOKLYN until the age of five. What he remembers of that time are the garbage bags in front of his family's railroad apartment. When he brought his English wife to America twenty years later, she refused to visit Central Park because of the muggers, addicts, and rapists. Instead, he told her that he would take her to another park, just as pretty, but safer. I have a photograph of her on that first visit to Central Park, reaching up through the delicate fretwork to a blossoming cherry. Had someone told my mother then that her future daughter would one day make her home in Brooklyn, on the edge of Frederick Law Olmsted's other, wilder park, she might have fled New York altogether—in those days, the notoriety of Prospect Park far outstripped even that of Central Park. As it was, my mother and father moved us out of Manhattan when I was three, to a new house with an old garden on Long Island. Planted in 1890, it was designed by the firm of the Olmsted Brothers, the sons of Frederick Olmsted. But unlike their father's most famous creations, this garden—our garden—remained largely untouched by violence.

[3]

NOWADAYS, PROSPECT PARK, too, feels untouched by violence. On summer days, when Long Meadow is full of sun-drunk children and picnickers, and the sky above is decorated with kites, few likely remember the grim days of the 1970s when the park was the lawless zone of a bankrupt city. Fewer still—only a lone man combing the grass with a metal detector, perhaps—might recall that a thousand American soldiers died here in the first and largest battle of the Revolutionary War. But under this verdant lawn there are still bullets to be found, and a few hundred feet away is the small wooded hill where, in 1776, American soldiers, led by General Sullivan, awaited the arrival of the British. They expected them from the south, on the road linking the village of Flatbush to the town of Brooklyn, and felled a giant white oak to create a blockade. It was a naïve and simple plan, and the hill now seems equally mild, more like the sort of kindly hump that children might scamper up for a game of king of the hill than a theater of war. The only troops that can be spotted on the road below, now the park's East Drive, are the clouds of cyclists that buzz past on weekend mornings. Yet this is where the first Americans waited to defend their freedom, unaware that behind them fourteen thousand British soldiers had slipped through an unguarded pass in Queen's County. Attacked from three sides, hundreds of Continental soldiers were staked with bayonets to these trees, and many more killed by carbines and cannon fire.

The grisly Battle of Brooklyn was lost, but just how fully realized those fallen soldiers' bid became is evident on a walk through Prospect Park on any day of the year. Quiet millions come to enjoy their portion of peace here, and though none of their expressions are exactly the same, there seems to be a common reflection in their faces. In an 1866 report by the park's landscape architects, one discovers the words for it: a "sense of enlarged freedom." That, wrote Frederick Law Olmsted and Calvert Vaux, was "to all, at all times, the most certain and the most valuable gratification afforded by a park." However universal their meaning, those words were written as the earliest excavations for the park's creation were turning up the bones of the Revolutionary War soldiers—those who fought for the freedom that later others were given to enlarge.

[4]

IT MAY BE THAT ALL PARKS tender freedom, but some serve up more than others. Hampstead Heath, for example, offers a greater helping than St. James Park, and the Bois de Boulogne offers more freedom than the Jardin du Luxembourg (where the forbidden grass is policed by gendarmes). It isn't only a question of greater acreage, where there is more chance of becoming lost or feeling alone. It's also a looseness of form—what is called wildness because it is not tamed into rows, herded into symmetry, pruned to the shape of an exacting idea, or in any other way limited. Such parks usually have wooded regions, where the processes of life—death, decay, new growth—are allowed to occur unimpeded. The definition of beauty is wider in these places, more generous. This looseness is visible, but it's also felt in spirit. If the plants are left to pursue their own designs, so, too, it usually follows, are the visitors.

Central Park is large and gracious, but is kept from such looseness by the fact that it is surrounded by the tightest of grids, and is the crowning gem of a wealthy, glamorous, and ambitious city that grooms its every acre. It may come as no surprise that Olmsted and Vaux had to bend to overbearing and demanding commissioners during the park's design and construction in the 1850s. In the end, frustration drove Olmsted to abandon the Central Park job and flee to California. He only agreed to return for the new park in Brooklyn because he and Vaux were promised complete liberty in the design. The result is one of the very wildest and most rugged city parks to be found anywhere. Neglected, abandoned, sometimes forgotten, Prospect Park became wilder still over the years. But even now, restored through the impassioned efforts of an alliance of neighbors, the park retains a sense of the untamable. At its center is a large swath of woods where one really can get lost. And there are still corners, like the dilapidated but beautiful Vale of Cashmere, whose silent abandon reminds one that nature will always have the last say.

[5]

THE WEATHER IN THE PARK is always more notable than the weather outside of it, both stranger and more extreme. Fifty thousand years ago, the park was buried under a sheet of ice a thousand feet thick. (When the Wisconsin glacier began to recede, it left behind a ridge of rocks, sediment, and soil it had dragged along. This terminal moraine became the woodlands, the ravine, and the hills of Long Meadow.) Is there something in this history that might explain the low and ghostly fog that fills the meadow on certain spring or fall mornings? (Many times we've lost our dog in it.) Or how, after a heavy rain, the same meadow floods significantly enough that seagulls appear from miles away, and scream overhead? And what about the special winds that make the meadow the favorite spot of kite flyers? The West Indians make their own from FedEx packages, a habit learned from their Easter celebrations of the resurrection of Christ. They send them as high as helicopters, whose propellers occasionally slice their strings.

Even weather shared with the surrounding area is expressed more dramatically here. Lightning storms and occasional hurricanes (and once even a tornado) leave the park littered with downed trees and splintered branches. Cleanup is always slow, and not all the debris is removed—whether it's due to lack of money, or the park's spirit of wildness, is hard to say; most likely, some of both. The fallen trees left to lie are claimed by children, who use them as balance beams, ships, or forts.

And of course, snow stays longer here than anywhere else. For days, and sometimes weeks, Long Meadow turns Flemish, as if painted by Brueghel: hundreds of miniatures in colored woolens, sledding and making merry.

[6]

FIRST THE DOGS, BUT, FINALLY, the birds. There are long stretches of night, dawn, and dusk, that belong mostly to them. After the park's watercourse was restored a decade ago, they began to return in large numbers. When my oldest son was a baby, we watched a red-tailed hawk devour a squirrel just a few feet away from us, near the Third Street Playground. He and I are still in the habit of reporting to each other the birds of prey we've spotted on our separate walks in the park. Once, alone with the dog on a gray morning, another red-tailed hawk glided just above me with a mouse in its talons. It's difficult to describe the sound overhead, how one knows they're there: as if a deeper shade of silence has been injected into the atmosphere.

And then they are gone, and one turns one's attention to the other forms of wildlife that have flourished here in recent years: cyclists, ball players, babies, Russians from the local home for the elderly, Orthodox Jews in fur Sabbath *shtreimels*, wedding parties, landscape painters, tai chi masters, old married couples, and every other sort of native species.

PHOTOGRAPHER'S NOTES

DURING MY CHILDHOOD, I spent a lot of summers at my grandfather's country house falling in love with gardening, learning about trees, flowers, vegetables, and dogs. In my mind, the concept of a garden became private and personal. Back in the city for school, I was obliged by my mother to go to the Valentino, a public park in Turin. What a waste of time, I would think, to stroll in a place that isn't private but belongs to everyone. So, growing up, my experience with public gardens became associated with negative memories. The idea of photographing them was never something I thought about, but things drastically changed one evening in December.

DECEMBER 9, 2011   Catie invites me for a drink to discuss a possible idea. "I think we should explore the possibility of making an essay on public parks around the world," she tells me in the most gracious way. After one more sip of delicious white wine, I am totally drawn into the project by my curiosity.

DECEMBER 10, 2011   I put my bad memories aside and I drive with Dee, Catie's friend, to Prospect Park in Brooklyn, the first subject of an adventure that will make me feel like a modern Phileas Fogg, a Jules Verne character. The kings and queens of Prospect Park are hundreds of preppy dogs who don't bark, don't growl, follow the rules, and make their masters incidental.

JANUARY 4, 2012   The Boboli Gardens are beautiful this crisp, freezing morning. The oaks, cypresses, bust, and fountains are my only companions.

JANUARY 8, 2012   I enter the Tiergarten through Brandenburg Gate. The park is lonely in winter. The Duke of Prussia may still be hunting there and I feel surrounded by thousands of dead Russian soldiers.

JANUARY 24–26, 2012   Polar temperature in Moscow and St. Petersburg. Every road of Gorky Park is turned into a skate track, packs of dogs run wild in the snowy fields, the benches at Kirov Park are empty, Tsarskoe Selo is silent and still.

FEBRUARY 11, 2012   It is warm at al-Azhar in Cairo. Young kids cut school for the day to use the park as a flirting ground. Security guards stop anything beyond an innocent glance.

MARCH 29, 2012   Young people flirt at Dumbarton Oaks surrounded by the beauty of the cherry blossoms. Older people take a botanical stroll.

MARCH 31, 2012   The garden of Xochimilco in Mexico City is a feast of music, food, dance, color, and flowers.

APRIL 27, 2012   I walk the Villa Borghese gardens imagining the beauty of past centuries.

MAY 2, 2012   Is my walk with Catie at the High Line in Manhattan. No matter what time of the year, I feel as though I am on the runway of a fashion show.

MAY 23, 2012   It is raining at Park Güell in Barcelona; still people take their turn to be photographed on the Gaudí steps.

JUNE 16, 2012   Grant and Lincoln Parks in Chicago are the perfect marriage between architecture and landscape. Everybody is full of energy.

JUNE 20, 2012   The day before a *Vogue* shoot I take a walk in the Luxembourg Gardens. I try to take a spin on the merry-go-round, but I am not allowed.

JUNE 28, 2012   Hyde Park in London is the perfect park: grass, flowers, lakes, trees, lovers, joggers, drug users, dogs, pears, kids, make up a Hockney painting.

AUGUST 10, 2012 In the small public garden of Trieste I find multitude of busts, reminding me of my high school studies.

SEPTEMBER 28, 2012 I meet with Andrew Sean Greer to take a tour of the Presidio in San Francisco. "Everybody is naked and makes love on the beaches," he tells me. Unfortunately, it was a foggy and freezing day so I had to postpone that vision.

SEPTEMBER 29, 2012 The view from the observatory at Griffith Park in Los Angeles is amazing.

OCTOBER 20–29, 2012 The longest trip of my life. In Kyoto I visit Maruyama Park: in three days I saw just a couple of cats so I decided that dogs are not very popular there. On the contrary, a multitude of geishas and worshippers praying at the dozens of temples scattered around the mountain.

Sheep, dogs, crows, and young Indians playing cricket are the inhabitants of the Maidan in Kolkata. The dogs are not preppy, but have great dignity. They walk silently without showing any emotion, searching for food. Misery is silent, but doesn't kill your pride. The only noise you hear comes from the crows at sunset.

After a long flight I arrive in Dublin. Cold and rain are the perfect weather for Iveagh Garden.

THESE AREN'T EVEN ALL MY EXPERIENCES, but they are enough to have changed my judgment on public gardens: magical places where you don't have to push the lawn mower, prune, plant, or weed. You can simply enjoy the beauty of nature and the variety of people. Feel the history. Experience the emotions.

It took me sixty-six years to realize that my mother was right; and thank you, Catie, for making this possible.

— OBERTO GILI

ACKNOWLEDGMENTS

THIS BOOK HAS BEEN a wonderful group effort from my Parks Department—as charmingly coined by David Lida. I've loved the collegial spirit of so many special people contributing from far-flung places to make this book come together.

From the day I first met Oberto, almost twenty years ago, I knew it would be a great pleasure to know him. That has been proven to be all the more true during the last year. He has talent, curiosity, goodwill, a generous spirit, and humor in abundance. Working with him has been a joy.

My gratitude to my agent, Lynn Nesbit, and my editor, Jonathan Burnham, knows no bounds. Lynn Nesbit, my long-standing friend and now my agent, helped from start to finish with wise counsel, creative editorial ideas, and unflagging, caring support. I see why she is so beloved by her writers. She also introduced me to her colleague Michael Steger, who persevered with good humor and the expertise to ensure the participation of all the writers.

Jonathan Burnham is the editor of my dreams. It's been a recurring and most pleasurable coincidence that each idea he has, every email he sends, makes me immediately nod and think "of course." I look back at where we started and realize what a huge difference his guidance has made to a project so close to my heart. He works with erudition, eloquence, grace, and kindness.

It's been a privilege to work with the illustrious group of writers involved. Each time an essay arrived, it was like receiving a wonderful present I could savor forever.

Designing this book has been a great team effort by Jonathan, Oberto, Mary Shanahan, and me. Mary has been our guiding hand. She is an exceptionally talented designer who has been a huge delight to work with. Even though she lives three thousand miles away, I felt as if she were down the street.

I am deeply grateful to many people who've helped me with their minds and hearts. My wholehearted thanks to:

Maya Ziv of HarperCollins. Her thoughtful, enthusiastic, and wise editorial work has enhanced this book.

Anna Wintour. Among the many people I've consulted for ideas on writers, she stands out.

My friends whom I know from my work for the New York Public Library. How lucky I was to meet with legendary editor Bob Silvers early on and benefit from his encouragement and wealth of knowledge along the way. Paul Holdengräber used his inventive mind to bounce around ideas with me and lead me to key writers. Thanks also to Dr. Judith Ginsberg, Dr. Paul LeClerc, David Remnick, Joshua Steiner, and Jean Strouse.

All the people who brainstormed with me, and especially to the following experts in their fields: Miranda Brooks, Adele Chatfield-Taylor, Henry Finder, Alma Guillermoprieto, Shirley Lord, Glenn Lowry, Charlie Rose, Dee Salomon, John Sexton, Ellyn Toscano, and Lord Weidenfeld. Special thanks to Doug Band.

Steve Rinehart, Ann Marie Kuder, David Young, and Hamid Najeddine.

THIS BOOK OWES ITS very existence to my husband, Don. I share many happy memories of walks in many of these parks with him and our children, William and Serena. This is a gift of my heart to them.

— CATIE MARRON

ABOUT THE CONTRIBUTORS

ANDRÉ ACIMAN is the chair of the Ph.D. Program in Comparative Literature at the CUNY Graduate Center and the director of the Writers' Institute. He is the author of *Out of Egypt, Alibis, Call Me by Your Name*, and most recently *Harvard Square*.

JONATHAN ALTER, born in Chicago in 1957, is a historian, journalist, and political analyst. He is the author of *The Defining Moment: FDR's Hundred Days and the Triumph of Hope, The Promise: President Obama, Year One*, and *The Center Holds: Obama and His Enemies*. For nearly three decades he was a reporter, editor, and columnist for *Newsweek*, and currently writes a column for Bloomberg View. He also appears as a contributor on NBC News and MSNBC. He lives with his family in Montclair, New Jersey.

JOHN BANVILLE'S novels include *The Sea, The Infinities*, and, most recently, *Ancient Light*. His latest crime novel under the pen name Benjamin Black is *Vengeance*. He lives in Dublin.

CANDICE BERGEN has made more than thirty films, but is probably best known for her role on the critically acclaimed CBS comedy *Murphy Brown*. During the show's ten-year run, Ms. Bergen received five Emmy Awards and two Golden Globe awards. She appeared on the critically acclaimed series *Boston Legal* and recently appeared on Broadway in *The Best Man*.

WILLIAM JEFFERSON CLINTON was the forty-second President of the United States.

AMANDA FOREMAN is the award-winning historian and internationally bestselling author of *Georgiana: Duchess of Devonshire* and *A World on Fire: Britain's Crucial Role in the American Civil War*. She is the recipient of the 1998 Whitbread Award for Biography and the 2011 Fletcher Pratt Award for Civil War History.

NORMAN FOSTER is chairman and founder of Foster + Partners, an international architectural practice. His projects include the transformation of the Reichstag in Berlin as a new Parliament. His numerous honors include the Knight Commander's Cross of the Order of Merit of the Federal Republic of Germany, the Pritzker Prize, the Praemium Imperiale, and a Life Peerage and Order of Merit bestowed by the Queen of the United Kingdom.

IAN FRAZIER writes nonfiction, essays, and humor. His books include *Great Plains*, *On the Rez*, and *Travels in Siberia*. Recently he published a comic novel, *The Cursing Mommy's Book of Days*. A longtime contributor to *The New Yorker*, he lives in Montclair, New Jersey.

ANDREW SEAN GREER is the bestselling author of five works of fiction, including *The Story of a Marriage* and *The Confessions of Max Tivol*. He is the recipient of the Northern California Book Award, the California Book Award, the New York Public Library Young Lions Award, the O. Henry Award for short fiction, and fellowships from the National Endowment for the Arts and the New York Public Library. Greer lives in San Francisco. His latest novel is *The Impossible Lives of Greta Wells*.

AMANDA HARLECH was born in London, grew up in Regent's Park, and now resides in Shropshire, England. A scholar at Oxford, she gained a degree in English language and literature. A creative consultant and cultural muse at Chanel, spending large periods of time in Paris, as well as being a consultant for Fendi, Amanda is at work on her first novel.

PICO IYER is the author of two novels and eight works of nonfiction, including *Video Night in Kathmandu*, *The Global Soul*, *The Open Road*, and, about his first year in Kyoto, *The Lady and the Monk*. He has been living in and around Kyoto since 1987.

NICOLE KRAUSS is the internationally bestselling author of *Great House*, *The History of Love*, and *Man Walks Into a Room*. Her books have been translated into more than thirty-five languages. She lives in Brooklyn, New York.

DAVID LIDA is the author of several books, among them *First Stop in the New World: Mexico City, the Capital of the 21st Century*, and *Las llaves de la ciudad*. When he is not writing, he works as an investigator for lawyers in the United States who defend Mexicans who are facing the death penalty. His website, Mostly Mexico City, can be found at www.davidlida.com.

JAN MORRIS, who is Anglo-Welsh and lives in Wales, was born in 1926 and has published some forty books of history, travel, biography, memoir, and fiction. She has frequented Trieste since the end of the Second World War and is the author of *Trieste and the Meaning of Nowhere*.

ZADIE SMITH is the author of the novels *White Teeth*, *The Autograph Man*, *On Beauty*, and *NW*, and the essay collection *Changing My Mind*. She is a professor of creative writing at New York University and a fellow of the Royal Society of Literature.

AHDAF SOUEIF's *The Map of Love* was short-listed for the Booker Prize and translated into thirty languages. Her most recent books are her memoir *Cairo: My City, Our Revolution* and, as editor, *Reflections on Islamic Art*. She is founder and chair of the Palestine Festival of Literature (PalFest).

COLM TÓIBÍN is the author of seven novels, including *The Master* and *Brooklyn*. His nonfiction includes *Homage to Barcelona*. He is a contributing editor at the *London Review of Books* and Irene and Sidney B. Silverman Professor in English and Comparative Literature at Columbia University. His books have been translated into thirty languages.

SIMON WINCHESTER, the author of some twenty-five works of nonfiction, was *The Guardian*'s South Asia correspondent, based in New Delhi, from 1976 to 1979. He currently lives in New York City and on a farm in the Berkshire Hills of western Massachusetts; his next book is *The Men Who United the States*.

ABOUT THE CREATORS

CATIE MARRON's career has included investment banking, magazine journalism, and public service. She is currently co-chair of the board of directors of Friends of the High Line; a trustee of The New York Public Library, where she was chairman of the board for seven years; and a contributing editor of *Vogue* magazine, along with other involvements.

OBERTO GILI is a photographer who specializes in shooting interiors and fashion. The author of *Home Sweet Home: Sumptuous and Bohemian Interiors* and *Luxury of Space*, he works for such publications as the *Wall Street Journal*, *Architectural Digest*, *Travel & Leisure*, and British, Spanish, and American *Vogue*. His website can be found at www.obertogili.com.